I0459253

SOCIAL SAVVINESS FOR TEENS AND YOUNG ADULTS

A Modern Guide to Overcoming
Social Media Traps, Anxiety,
Peer Pressure, and the Fear
of Missing Out.

NICCI BROCHARD
&
DR. BEN CHUBA

SOCIAL SAVVINESS FOR TEENS AND YOUNG ADULTS

A Modern Guide to Overcoming
Social Media Traps, Anxiety,
Peer Pressure, and the Fear
of Missing Out.

Copyright©2025

All rights reserved by Nicci Brochard and Dr. Ben Chuba

Published in the United States by Cross Border Publishers.

No part of this publication may be reproduced, stored, or transmitted in any form or by any means electronic, mechanical, photocopying, recording, or otherwise without prior written permission from the author or publisher, except for brief excerpts used in reviews or educational purposes as permitted by law.

This book is protected under U.S. and international copyright laws. Unauthorized reproduction, distribution, or adaptation of any portion of this work may result in legal consequences.

For permissions, licensing, or inquiries, please contact

info@crossborderpublishers.com: www.crossborderpublishers.com

Book Formatting by: *Monish*

Book cover design by: *Billy Design*

CROSSBORDER

New York, London, Quebec

Also published by Nicci Brochard and Dr. Ben Chuba

CONTENTS

PROLOGUE

Jane: Ugh. I swear, I need a break from social media.

Jordan: What happened now?

Jane: Nothing new. Just the usual: everyone posting their perfect lives, making me feel like I am missing out on everything. Trips to Europe, concert tickets, friend groups looking like they are straight out of a movie... Meanwhile, I'm sitting here with my cold coffee and an unfinished essay.

Jordan: I get it. It's like, even when I'm doing something cool, I'm worried about capturing the *perfect* post instead of just enjoying the moment.

Jane: Right? And then there's the pressure: if you don't post enough, people think you're irrelevant. If you post too much, you're "trying too hard." If you don't like or comment on your friends' stuff, they take it personally. It's exhausting!

Jordan: And don't even get me started on those influencers. They make it seem like if you're not traveling, dressing in designer clothes, or waking up at 5 AM for some "hustle culture" routine, you're failing at life.

Jane: Exactly! I know it's not real, but it *feels* real. And it messes with my head.

Jordan: You know what? There should be a guide for this stuff. Like, a real, no-nonsense guide on how to survive social media without losing your mind.

Jane: Yeah. How to handle peer pressure, avoid the comparison trap, deal with anxiety, and actually be happy *offline* too.

Jordan: If only that existed…

Jane: Maybe it does. Maybe it's right here in this book.

Nicci and I (Ben) want to thank you in advance for reading this book. We hope you find in it what you are looking for.

CHAPTER 1

THE DIGITAL AGE DILEMMA: UNDERSTANDING THE SOCIAL LANDSCAPE

"We live in a world where we are more connected than ever before, yet many feel more alone than ever."

— Ching L

The Evolution of Social Interaction: From Face-to-Face to Digital-First Communication

For centuries, human connections thrived on face-to-face interaction. Conversations unfolded in real-time, expressions were interpreted instinctively, and relationships were built on tangible experiences. From gathering around a fire to share stories to meeting at town squares, socializing was rooted in direct engagement.

Then came the telegraph, the telephone, and eventually, the internet, each milestone reshaping the way we communicate. However, the true revolution occurred with the advent of social media and instant messaging, shifting the paradigm from in-person interactions to digital-first connections.

Today, a majority of our interactions begin, evolve, and even dissolve within the confines of screens. Digital platforms have given us the ability to maintain global friendships, conduct business across continents, and share thoughts with the world in seconds. This shift, however, brings both profound benefits and unique challenges that previous generations never faced. While we celebrate the convenience, we must also grapple with the implications of a world where likes and follows often hold more weight than handshakes and hugs.

How Social Media Shapes Friendships, Perceptions, and Self-Worth

Social media has become an extension of our identities, influencing how we perceive ourselves and others. Platforms like Instagram, TikTok, and Twitter create an environment where friendships are measured in numbers, interactions are carefully curated, and validation is often sought through virtual approval.

Friendships, once built on mutual experiences and genuine conversations, are now frequently defined by engagement metrics. A friend's value can be unconsciously linked to how often they comment on posts or how quickly they respond to messages. The lines between true companionship and digital acquaintance blur, creating an environment where people may feel pressure to maintain relationships for appearance rather than genuine connection.

Beyond friendships, the digital space profoundly shapes self-worth. The pressure to present a picture-perfect life fuels a comparison culture, where individuals measure their happiness, beauty, and success against curated highlights of others. The rise of filters and photo-editing software exacerbates unrealistic standards, making it easy to forget that what we see online is often a polished illusion rather than an unfiltered reality.

The Double-Edged Sword of Connectivity: Advantages and Hidden Pitfalls

Digital connectivity is a powerful tool. It allows for instant communication across the world, democratizes information, and fosters communities that transcend geographical boundaries. The advantages are undeniable:

- **Accessibility:** Information is at our fingertips, making education and self-improvement more attainable than ever.
- **Networking:** Opportunities for career growth, learning, and collaboration expand exponentially in a connected world.
- **Support Systems:** Online communities provide solace, advice, and encouragement, particularly for those who may feel isolated in their physical surroundings.

Yet, with these benefits come significant pitfalls:

- **Superficiality:** Conversations can become transactional, focused more on maintaining an online presence than fostering meaningful dialogue.
- **Digital Fatigue:** Constant notifications, the pressure to be available, and the need to stay updated can lead to mental exhaustion.
- **Echo Chambers:** Algorithms often reinforce pre-existing beliefs, limiting exposure to diverse perspectives and fostering polarization.

The challenge, then, is to harness the positive aspects of digital connectivity while mitigating its downsides. Recognizing these dynamics is the first step toward developing a healthier relationship with technology.

Recognizing the Difference Between Authentic Interaction and Curated Online Personas

One of the greatest paradoxes of the digital age is that while social media is designed to connect us, it often promotes an illusion rather than reality. Online, people curate their lives to highlight the best moments while omitting struggles, failures, or mundane realities. This creates a skewed perception of life, making it easy to feel inadequate or left behind.

The distinction between authentic interaction and a carefully crafted online persona is crucial in maintaining mental and emotional well-being.

- **Authentic interactions** involve honest communication, vulnerability, and a willingness to share both successes and setbacks.
- **Curated personas** often prioritize image over substance, seeking validation through engagement rather than genuine connection.

Understanding this difference allows individuals to engage with social media more mindfully, reducing the impact of comparison and fostering a more balanced perspective on life.

Setting the Stage for Building Awareness and Confidence in a Hyper-Connected World

In a society where digital interactions dominate, self-awareness is key to navigating social landscapes without losing one's sense of self. The goal is not to reject technology but to develop a balanced, informed, and confident approach to digital engagement.

- **Mindful Consumption:** Being conscious of how much time is spent online and the emotional effects of digital interactions.
- **Digital Boundaries:** Establishing limits on screen time, social media usage, and the weight given to online validation.
- **Genuine Connections:** Prioritizing meaningful conversations and relationships, both online and offline.
- **Self-Confidence Beyond Metrics:** Understanding that self-worth is not determined by likes, followers, or viral success but by personal growth, character, and real-life impact.

As we move forward, the challenge is not merely adapting to the digital world but mastering it in a way that serves rather than controls us. By fostering awareness, embracing authenticity, and valuing genuine human connection, we can transform the digital landscape into a space that enhances rather than diminishes our social experiences.

THE FOMO EPIDEMIC: BREAKING THE CYCLE OF COMPARISON

"Comparison is the thief of joy." Theodore Roosevelt

Understanding Fear of Missing Out (FOMO) and Its Psychological Effects

Imagine scrolling through your phone late at night, only to see photos of your friends at an event you weren't invited to. A sinking feeling creeps in. Am I missing out on something important? This uneasy sensation is known as the Fear of Missing Out, or FOMO. It's a modern psychological phenomenon that triggers anxiety, envy, and self-doubt.

FOMO is more than just a fleeting emotion; it is deeply rooted in human psychology. Evolutionary, humans thrived in groups, relying on social connections for survival. Being excluded from the group in ancient times could mean a loss of protection and resources, making our brains highly sensitive to signs of exclusion. Fast forward to the digital age, and our brains still react to social exclusion with the same intensity. The difference now is that we are constantly bombarded with glimpses of others' curated lives, making it harder than ever to avoid comparison.

This phenomenon isn't just about social events. It extends to career choices, financial status, lifestyle, and even personal achievements. We see people buying homes, landing promotions, traveling to exotic locations, and it can feel like everyone else is moving forward while we remain stagnant. This relentless comparison can lead to dissatisfaction, anxiety, and, in extreme cases, even depression.

How Social Media Magnifies Feelings of Exclusion and Self-Doubt

Social media is a double-edged sword. On the one hand, it connects us with friends, allows us to share milestones, and provides entertainment. On the other, it fuels FOMO by offering an endless stream of images and stories showcasing the best moments of others' lives. What we often forget is that social media is a highlight reel, not an accurate depiction of reality.

Studies have shown that excessive social media use correlates with increased feelings of loneliness and inadequacy. Platforms like Instagram, TikTok, and Facebook employ algorithms that prioritize engaging content, often the most glamorous and exciting moments of people's lives. This selective exposure skews our perception of reality, making it seem like everyone else is living a more exciting and fulfilling life than we are.

Additionally, the illusion of constant fun and success can lead to a distorted self-image. When people post their achievements and experiences, we naturally compare them to our everyday lives, forgetting that struggles, failures, and mundane moments are rarely shared online. This fuels self-doubt and leads to the dangerous belief that we are falling behind.

Strategies to Shift from Comparison to Contentment

Overcoming FOMO requires a shift in perspective. Here are some effective strategies to help break the cycle of comparison and cultivate a sense of contentment:

1. **Curate Your Social Media Feed** Be intentional about the content you consume. Unfollow accounts that trigger feelings of inadequacy or comparison. Instead, follow pages that inspire and

uplift you. Consider setting screen-time limits to reduce excessive scrolling and allow yourself more time for meaningful offline activities.

2. **Practice Digital Detoxing** Take regular breaks from social media. Try a 24-hour detox once a week or reduce your screen time gradually. Use this time to engage in hobbies, connect with loved ones in person, or simply enjoy moments of solitude.

3. **Reframe Your Mindset** When you catch yourself comparing your life to someone else's, remind yourself that social media does not reflect reality. Consciously reframe thoughts of envy into thoughts of appreciation. Instead of thinking, "Why am I not there?" try thinking, "I'm glad they had a great time, and I can create my own joy too."

4. **Engage in Activities That Bring You Joy** FOMO often arises when we feel unfulfilled in our own lives. Identify activities that make you genuinely happy and prioritize them. Whether it's reading, painting, exercising, or spending time with loved ones, engaging in activities that bring personal satisfaction diminishes the desire to compare yourself to others.

5. **Set Personal Goals** Shift your focus from external validation to personal growth. Set realistic and meaningful goals that align with your values and aspirations. Celebrate small victories along the way, and remind yourself that progress is personal, not comparative.

Developing a Balanced Perspective on Social Events and Online Experiences

While FOMO often stems from social media, it also affects real-life situations. We may feel pressured to attend every social gathering, fearing that missing out will damage our relationships or social status. However, developing a balanced perspective can help mitigate these feelings.

1. **Prioritize Meaningful Connections** Not every event or gathering is essential. Instead of saying yes to everything out of fear, prioritize events that align with your interests and bring value to your life. Quality over quantity matters when it comes to relationships and experiences.

2. **Embrace JOMO (Joy of Missing Out)** The opposite of FOMO, JOMO is the practice of appreciating and enjoying the present moment, even when you choose to opt out of certain experiences. It's about recognizing that missing an event does not equate to missing out on life. Finding joy in solitude or intentional rest is a powerful counter to FOMO.

3. **Understand That No One Has It All** Just as you experience FOMO while looking at others' lives, others experience it looking at yours. Everyone has their struggles and insecurities, even if they are not visible online. Remembering this can help put things in perspective and alleviate feelings of exclusion.

Practical Exercises to Cultivate Gratitude and Self-Appreciation

To solidify a mindset, shift away from comparison and towards contentment, incorporating practical exercises can be incredibly effective:

1. **Daily Gratitude Journaling** Each morning or evening, write down three things you are grateful for. These can be as simple as a good cup of coffee, a meaningful conversation, or progress in a personal goal. Over time, this practice rewires your brain to focus on abundance rather than lack.

2. **Mindfulness and Meditation** Practicing mindfulness helps you stay present and appreciate your current reality rather than being consumed by thoughts of what others are doing. Meditation, even for just a few minutes a day, can help reduce anxiety associated with FOMO and increase overall contentment.

3. **Affirmations for Self-Worth** Create and recite affirmations that reinforce your self-worth. Statements like "I am enough," "I choose to appreciate my journey," and "My value is not defined by social media" can help counter negative self-talk.

4. **Create a Reverse Bucket List** Instead of listing things you wish to do, make a list of things you have already accomplished and enjoyed. Reflecting on past experiences can help shift focus from what you lack to what you have gained.

5. **Spend More Time in the Present** Engage in activities that encourage presence, such as hiking, reading, playing an instrument, or simply taking a walk without your phone. The more you practice being in the moment, the less you worry about what others are doing.

Conclusion

FOMO is a powerful force in today's hyper-connected world, but it does not have to dictate your happiness. By understanding its psychological roots, being mindful of social media's impact, and actively practicing gratitude and self-appreciation, you can break free from the cycle of comparison. Life is not a competition, and fulfillment comes from appreciating what we have rather than longing for what we think we're missing.

So, the next time you feel that familiar pang of FOMO creeping in, take a deep breath, remind yourself that your journey is unique, and find joy in the present moment. Because in the end, true happiness is not found in comparison, but in contentment.

CHAPTER 3

SOCIAL ANXIETY IN THE DIGITAL ERA: CONQUERING FEAR AND SELF-DOUBT

"We are becoming the tools of our tools."

– Henry David Thoreau

In this day and age where digital communication is more prevalent than ever, one might assume that social confidence has increased alongside it. However, paradoxically, the rise of online interactions has given birth to new challenges in face-to-face communication, often exacerbating social anxiety rather than alleviating it. This chapter explores the impact of digital interactions on real-world confidence, the paradox of connectivity, recognizing and managing social anxiety triggers, and practical techniques to enhance social skills in an era dominated by screens.

How Online Interactions Impact Real-World Social Confidence

Digital platforms have revolutionized the way people interact. Social media, messaging apps, and virtual meetings offer convenience and accessibility, enabling connections across vast distances. However, these virtual interactions often come at a cost: reduced confidence in real-world social situations.

Online communication allows individuals to carefully curate their responses, edit messages, and avoid the discomfort of spontaneous conversations. This creates an illusion of social mastery, where users feel in control of interactions but struggle with unfiltered, real-time exchanges in person. As a result, many people who rely heavily on digital communication may feel anxiety when faced with direct social interactions, fearing awkward silences, misinterpretations, or judgment.

Another significant factor is the reduced exposure to nonverbal cues. In face-to-face conversations, body language, tone of voice, and facial expressions contribute significantly to communication. Digital communication often lacks these elements, making it difficult to develop the skills necessary for interpreting and responding to nonverbal cues in real-world interactions. Consequently, individuals who spend excessive time communicating online may find in-person socialization more daunting and unpredictable.

The Paradox of Connectivity: Why More Communication Doesn't Always Mean Deeper Relationships

Technology has made it easier to stay in touch with friends, family, and colleagues. However, this increased connectivity does not necessarily translate to deeper, more meaningful relationships. Many people experience a paradox where they are more connected than ever yet feel lonelier and more socially anxious.

One reason for this paradox is the superficial nature of many online interactions. A quick "like," comment, or emoji response on social media can create the illusion of engagement without fostering genuine emotional connection. Virtual conversations often lack depth, making it harder for individuals to develop the trust and vulnerability that are foundational to strong relationships.

Additionally, the abundance of digital communication options can lead to social comparison and fear of missing out (FOMO). Scrolling through curated highlight reels of other people's lives can intensify self-doubt and insecurity, making individuals more hesitant to engage socially in real life. Rather than boosting confidence, constant exposure to idealized versions of others' lives can heighten social anxiety, reinforcing the fear of being judged or not measuring up.

Recognizing and Managing Social Anxiety Triggers

To conquer social anxiety in the digital era, it is essential to recognize its triggers. Many people experience heightened social anxiety in situations that involve:

- **Real-Time Communication Pressure:** Instant messaging and live video calls can create anxiety due to the expectation of quick, articulate responses without the time to craft or edit thoughts.

- **Fear of Negative Judgment:** Social media exposes individuals to public scrutiny, where the fear of receiving criticism or negative feedback can amplify social anxiety.

- **Over-Reliance on Digital Validation:** Seeking likes, comments, and shares as indicators of self-worth can create a dependency on external validation, making real-world interactions feel more intimidating.

- **Avoidance Behavior:** The ease of online communication allows individuals to avoid challenging social situations in real life, reinforcing fears instead of overcoming them.

Managing these triggers involves setting boundaries with technology and developing strategies to build real-world confidence. Gradual exposure to in-person interactions, practicing mindfulness, and limiting social media comparisons are effective ways to regain control over social anxiety.

Techniques for Building Real-Life Social Skills Despite Digital Distractions

To cultivate social confidence, individuals must balance digital interactions with real-world experiences. The following techniques can help:

- **Face-to-Face Practice:** Prioritize in-person conversations whenever possible. Whether it's meeting a friend for coffee or engaging in small talk with a cashier, real-life interactions help build confidence.

- **Active Listening:** Practice focusing on what others are saying rather than worrying about how you will respond. Active listening fosters genuine connections and reduces self-consciousness.

- **Mindful Technology Use:** Set designated times for social media use and avoid excessive scrolling. Being mindful of online habits helps reduce digital dependency and encourages more meaningful real-world interactions.

- **Gradual Exposure:** If social interactions feel overwhelming, start with low-pressure environments, such as joining a casual group activity or attending a community event where participation is optional.

- **Improving Nonverbal Communication:** Work on maintaining eye contact, using open body language, and mirroring positive social cues to improve real-world social confidence.

Role-Playing Exercises to Practice Engaging Confidently in Various Settings

Role-playing can be an effective way to practice real-world social interactions in a controlled and supportive environment. Here are a few exercises:

1. **The Introduction Challenge:** Pair up with a friend or family member and practice introducing yourself in different settings, such as a networking event, a party, or a work meeting.

2. **Handling Awkward Silences:** Simulate a conversation where an intentional pause is inserted. Practice responding naturally by asking follow-up questions or sharing a personal anecdote.

3. **Public Speaking Practice:** Choose a topic and give a brief talk in front of a small group or even in front of a mirror. This helps reduce anxiety about speaking in front of others.

4. **Assertive Communication Exercise:** Practice setting boundaries and expressing opinions confidently in simulated scenarios, such as negotiating a deal or declining an invitation.

5. **Empathy and Perspective-Taking:** Engage in role-playing where you switch roles with another person to understand different perspectives in a conversation.

Conclusion

While the digital era has reshaped communication, it is still possible to build real-world confidence and social skills. By recognizing the limitations of online interactions, managing social anxiety triggers, and actively practicing face-to-face communication, individuals can reclaim their social confidence. Technology should serve as a tool for connection rather than a crutch that deepens social fears. By stepping outside the digital comfort zone and embracing real-world experiences, anyone can conquer fear and self-doubt, fostering stronger and more fulfilling relationships.

CHAPTER 4

PEER PRESSURE AND ONLINE INFLUENCE :STANDING STRONG IN YOUR VALUES

"Be yourself; everyone else is already taken."

— Oscar Wilde

In this day and age, social validation is often measured in likes, shares, and follows, the challenge of standing firm in one's values has never been more daunting. Peer pressure has always been a significant part of growing up, but the digital age has magnified its influence in unprecedented ways. Unlike the traditional face-to-face pressure of previous generations, today's youth must navigate an omnipresent, always-connected world where influence is just a click away.

The Evolution of Peer Pressure in the Digital Landscape

Peer pressure used to be limited to direct social interactions—a friend convincing another to try smoking behind the school, a group deciding what clothing brands are "cool," or students pressuring each other to conform to social norms. However, the rise of the internet and social media has drastically altered the way peer pressure operates. Today, the influence extends beyond a small circle of friends to an online audience of potentially thousands or even millions.

Social media platforms serve as both a stage and a magnifying glass, intensifying the impact of peer pressure. Influencers, celebrities, and everyday users alike curate and showcase their best moments, setting unrealistic expectations for behavior, appearance, and success. The pressure to conform is no longer just about impressing peers in a physical space; it is about gaining the approval of a digital audience.

Moreover, social media algorithms reinforce certain behaviors by pushing trending content to more users, making it appear as though everyone is engaging in the same activities. This creates a cycle where individuals feel compelled to join in, often without questioning whether the trend aligns with their personal values.

The Hidden Dangers of Viral Trends, Challenges, and Social Media Dares

It starts as a simple challenge: pour a bucket of ice water over your head for charity. But then, social media challenges evolve into riskier, sometimes dangerous stunts. While some trends serve a noble cause, many others prioritize shock value and attention over safety and common sense.

Viral challenges like the "Tide Pod Challenge," where participants consumed toxic laundry detergent, or the "Cinnamon Challenge," which involved swallowing a spoonful of cinnamon without water, highlight how online pressure can push individuals to compromise their safety for the sake of digital clout. These trends are often framed as fun and harmless, but they can have real-life consequences, from health risks to legal repercussions.

Psychologically, participating in these challenges often stems from a fear of missing out (FOMO). The fear that others are gaining popularity and status through participation makes it difficult for individuals to resist, even when they know the potential dangers.

Identifying Manipulation Tactics Used by Influencers, Brands, and Peers

Marketing, advertising, and influencer culture have perfected the art of persuasion. Brands use psychological triggers such as exclusivity, urgency, and social proof to influence buying decisions. Similarly, influencers use curated lifestyles, sponsorships, and personal anecdotes to shape audience behavior.

Some common manipulation tactics include:

- **Scarcity and Urgency:** Messages like "Only 24 hours left to buy!" or "Limited edition" create a sense of pressure that leads people to act impulsively.

- **Social Proof:** Seeing that an influencer or large group endorses a product or action makes it seem more acceptable or even necessary.

- **Emotional Appeals:** Influencers often use personal stories to create emotional connections, making their audience more likely to trust and follow their advice.

- **Comparison Culture:** Constant exposure to seemingly perfect lifestyles can lead to feelings of inadequacy and the desire to conform to unrealistic standards.

Understanding these tactics can help individuals make informed decisions rather than being swayed by deceptive online persuasion.

Setting Personal Boundaries and Staying True to Your Values

Establishing and maintaining personal boundaries is essential in resisting online peer pressure. This involves knowing your core values, setting limits on social media use, and practicing self-awareness.

Strategies to Stay Grounded:

1. **Know Your Values:** Clearly define what you stand for. Are you passionate about honesty, kindness, or authenticity? Keeping your values at the forefront makes it easier to resist pressure that contradicts them.

2. **Limit Social Media Exposure:** The more time spent online, the greater the exposure to peer pressure. Taking breaks and setting usage limits can reduce susceptibility.

3. **Be Selective with Influences:** Follow people who inspire, educate, and empower rather than those who make you feel inadequate or pressured to conform.

4. **Practice Mindful Consumption:** Before engaging with a trend or making a decision influenced by online content, ask yourself whether it aligns with your values.

5. **Develop a Support System:** Surround yourself with friends and family who respect your boundaries and encourage you to stay true to yourself.

How to Assert Yourself Confidently Without Fear of Social Rejection

One of the biggest fears surrounding peer pressure is social rejection. However, confidence in one's values and the ability to assert them respectfully can minimize this fear.

Effective Ways to Stand Your Ground:

- **Use "I" Statements:** Instead of saying, "That's a stupid challenge," say, "I don't feel comfortable participating in that."

- **Practice Saying No:** The more you practice refusing things that go against your values, the easier it becomes.

- **Redirect the Conversation:** If pressured to do something uncomfortable, change the topic or suggest a safer alternative.

- **Stay Firm but Respectful:** Confidence doesn't mean being confrontational. Express your opinions calmly and assertively.

- **Find Like-Minded Communities:** There are many online and offline groups that share similar values and can reinforce positive choices.

Ultimately, standing strong in the face of peer pressure, both online and offline, requires self-awareness, critical thinking, and confidence. By setting clear boundaries, recognizing manipulation tactics, and asserting one's values with assurance, individuals can navigate the digital landscape with integrity and independence. In a world driven by trends, staying true to oneself is the most powerful statement of all.

CHAPTER 5

THE MYTH OF PERFECTION: OVERCOMING THE NEED FOR ONLINE VALIDATION

The Allure of Digital Approval

In an era where social media dictates trends, opinions, and self-worth, the pursuit of perfection has taken center stage. The number of likes, comments, and shares on a post often feels like a public validation of one's value. But is this digital approval a genuine reflection of self-worth, or is it an illusion carefully crafted by algorithms and social expectations?

The Psychology Behind Likes, Comments, and Shares

The human brain is wired to seek social connection. Studies have shown that receiving likes and comments on social media activates the brain's reward system, releasing dopamine, the same chemical associated with pleasure and addiction. This neurological response creates a cycle where individuals continuously seek external approval to experience the same high, reinforcing a dependency on digital validation.

Moreover, the concept of "social comparison theory" suggests that people measure their worth based on how they compare to others. When scrolling through Instagram, TikTok, or Facebook, the curated highlights of others' lives can create an unrealistic benchmark for success and happiness. The absence of likes or comments can feel like rejection, amplifying insecurities and leading to a constant quest for approval.

How Algorithms Feed into Self-Worth Issues and Insecurity

Social media platforms are designed to keep users engaged. The more time people spend scrolling, the more advertisements they consume, benefiting the platform's revenue model. Algorithms play a crucial role in this process by tailoring content to individual preferences and rewarding engagement. However, this reinforcement loop comes at a cost of emotional dependence on digital validation.

Algorithms prioritize content that garners high engagement, creating an environment where people feel pressured to post what they believe will get the most interaction rather than what is authentic. This contributes to a "performance mindset," where individuals begin tailoring their online personas to fit the expectations of their audience rather than expressing their true selves. Over time, this manufactured identity can erode genuine self-esteem, leading to anxiety and an overwhelming fear of being perceived as inadequate.

The Dangers of Seeking External Validation Through Social Media

While social media can be a tool for connection and self-expression, an overreliance on external validation can have detrimental effects on mental health. Some of the dangers include:

- **Increased Anxiety and Depression:** Studies have linked excessive social media use to higher rates of anxiety and depression, often due to unrealistic comparisons and the pressure to maintain a curated image.

- **Loss of Authenticity:** When people prioritize validation over self-expression, they may suppress their true thoughts and feelings, leading to an identity crisis.

- **Fear of Missing Out (FOMO):** Seeing peers engaging in exciting experiences can make individuals feel like they are falling behind in life.

- **Reduced Real-Life Interactions:** The constant need to document and seek approval online can detract from meaningful in-person experiences.

Over time, this reliance on external approval can lead to a fragile sense of self-worth that fluctuates based on the response to each post. The more one chases perfection, the more distant true fulfillment becomes.

Shifting From a Performance Mindset to a Confident Identity

The key to breaking free from the cycle of online validation is shifting from a performance-driven mindset to a confident, self-assured identity. This transition requires self-awareness, intentionality, and a willingness to embrace imperfection. Here are some ways to make that shift:

1. **Reassess Your Relationship with social media:** Take a step back and evaluate how much time and energy you invest in seeking validation online. If a post's engagement (or lack thereof) significantly impacts your mood, it may be time to reconsider your priorities.

2. **Engage in Self-Reflection:** Instead of focusing on how others perceive you, focus on how you perceive yourself. Ask yourself: *Would I still do this if no one was watching?*

3. **Practice Digital Detoxes:** Setting boundaries with social media use, such as designating screen-free hours or taking periodic detoxes, can help break the cycle of dependency on digital validation.

4. **Focus on Real-Life Connections:** Genuine relationships are built on authenticity, not curated perfection. Prioritizing face-to-face interactions can provide a deeper sense of belonging than any number of likes ever could.

5. **Develop an Internal Validation System:** Cultivate self-worth by recognizing your intrinsic value. Engaging in activities that bring joy and fulfillment, without the need for external approval, helps build a resilient self-image.

Embracing Authenticity in Both Online and Offline Spaces

Authenticity is the antidote to the pressure of online perfection. When individuals embrace their true selves, both online and offline, they cultivate confidence that is not dependent on validation from others. Here are some ways to foster authenticity:

- **Share Real Moments:** Instead of only posting picture-perfect highlights, share moments that reflect your true experiences, including struggles and growth.

- **Follow Accounts That Inspire Authenticity:** Curate your feed to include creators and individuals who promote self-acceptance rather than unrealistic perfection.

- **Be Mindful of Your Intentions:** Before posting, ask yourself: *Am I sharing this because it resonates with me, or because I want validation?*

- **Accept Imperfection:** Perfection is an illusion. Embracing flaws and vulnerabilities fosters genuine connections and inner peace.

Conclusion

Social media is a powerful tool, but it should never define self-worth. The myth of perfection perpetuated by online validation is just that—a myth. By shifting from a performance mindset to a confident identity, individuals can reclaim their sense of self, free from the constraints of likes and comments. True confidence comes from within, and it thrives in authenticity, not in the pursuit of digital approval.

Ultimately, the most fulfilling validation is the kind that comes from living authentically, embracing imperfection, and cultivating self-worth beyond the screen. The moment you stop chasing online perfection, you start experiencing real-life fulfillment.

DIGITAL DETOX: TAKING BACK CONTROL OF YOUR ATTENTION AND TIME

The Weekend Without Wi-Fi

On a Friday evening, Jane found herself mindlessly scrolling through social media after a long workweek. The cycle was all too familiar: open Instagram, check Twitter, watch a few TikTok videos, and repeat. Suddenly, she realized that nearly two hours had passed, and she had accomplished nothing but consuming an endless stream of content. Frustrated, she decided to do something drastic. That weekend, she turned off her phone, stored away her laptop, and resolved to spend the next two days without any digital distractions. Initially, it felt uncomfortable, as if she were missing out on something vital. However, as the hours passed, she rediscovered simple joys: reading a book, going for a long walk, and having an uninterrupted conversation with a friend. By Sunday night, she felt a sense of clarity and peace she hadn't experienced in years. This small experiment made her realize just how much control technology had over her attention and time.

The Science Behind Social Media Addiction and Its Impact on Mental Health

The human brain is wired to seek pleasure, and social media exploits this natural tendency. Every like, comment, and notification trigger a release of dopamine, a neurotransmitter associated with reward and pleasure. Over time, our brains associate social media interactions with instant gratification, leading to compulsive behavior and an increased craving for digital validation.

Research indicates that excessive social media use is linked to heightened stress, anxiety, and even depression. A study published in *JAMA Pediatrics* found that teenagers who spend more than three hours a day on social media are at a higher risk of developing mental health issues. Furthermore, doomscrolling, endlessly consuming negative news—can amplify feelings of hopelessness and anxiety. The curated, often unrealistic portrayals of life on social platforms contribute to a distorted self-image and increased comparison, fueling dissatisfaction and lower self-esteem.

Additionally, the constant digital noise can impair cognitive functions, reducing our ability to focus and retain information. Studies suggest that multitasking between social media, emails, and other online activities can decrease productivity and increase cognitive fatigue.

Recognizing Signs of Over-Dependence on Technology

It's easy to overlook the extent of our digital dependence, but recognizing the warning signs is crucial. Some key indicators include:

- **Inability to focus without checking your phone**: If you find yourself reaching for your device within minutes of starting a task, you might be struggling with digital distraction.

- **Feeling anxious without your phone**: Experiencing restlessness or distress when your phone is out of reach is a red flag.

- **Using social media as an emotional crutch**: If you turn to scrolling whenever you feel bored, sad, or stressed, you might be using technology as a coping mechanism.

- **Neglecting real-world interactions**: Preferring virtual engagement over face-to-face conversations with friends and family can signal an unhealthy reliance on digital connections.

- **Frequent doomscrolling**: Continuously consuming negative content without feeling able to stop is a sign of digital overconsumption.

Practical Steps to Reduce Screen Time Without Feeling Disconnected

The idea of reducing screen time can feel overwhelming, especially in a hyper-connected world. However, small, intentional changes can make a significant difference. Here are some practical strategies:

1. **Set Screen Time Limits**: Use built-in phone features to track and limit your screen time. Set specific time constraints for apps that tend to consume most of your attention.

2. **Establish No-Phone Zones**: Designate certain areas of your home, such as the dining table and bedroom, as tech-free zones to encourage quality time with family and better sleep hygiene.

3. **Schedule Phone-Free Hours**: Implement a daily period where you intentionally disconnect from your devices. This could be during meals, in the morning, or before bed.

4. **Use the 20-Second Rule**: Make digital distractions less accessible by placing your phone in another room or enabling grayscale mode to make social media apps less appealing.

5. **Replace Digital Habits with Offline Activities**: Instead of reaching for your phone, engage in activities like journaling, reading, or exercising.

6. **Enable Do Not Disturb Mode**: Turn off non-essential notifications to reduce the impulse to check your phone constantly.

7. **Unfollow and Unsubscribe**: Curate your digital environment by unfollowing accounts that promote negativity or unnecessary distractions.

Mindful Social Media Habits for Healthier Engagement

Since social media is deeply embedded in modern life, the goal isn't necessarily to eliminate it but to engage with it more mindfully. Here are some ways to develop healthier digital habits:

- **Consume with intention**: Before opening an app, ask yourself why you're using it. Are you seeking information, entertainment, or connection? Being aware of your purpose can help curb mindless scrolling.

- **Set boundaries**: Limit your social media use to certain times of the day instead of checking it continuously.

- **Engage, don't just consume**: Instead of passively scrolling, interact with meaningful content, leave comments, and share valuable insights.

- **Follow accounts that inspire and uplift**: Curate your feed to include educational, motivational, and enriching content rather than content that fosters comparison and negativity.

- **Take regular detox breaks**: Consider taking weekly or monthly breaks from social media to reset your mind and focus on real-life experiences.

Finding Fulfillment in Offline Hobbies and Real-World Connections

One of the biggest concerns about reducing screen time is the fear of missing out (FOMO). However, replacing digital consumption with fulfilling offline activities can make the transition easier and more rewarding.

Reconnecting with Hobbies

Many people abandon hobbies due to the convenience of digital entertainment. Reconnecting with lost interests can reignite creativity and bring genuine joy. Consider activities such as:

- **Reading books**: Diving into a captivating book can be more rewarding than scrolling through endless social media posts.

- **Creative pursuits**: Painting, writing, playing a musical instrument, or crafting provide mental stimulation and a sense of accomplishment.

- **Physical activities**: Exercising, hiking, yoga, and dancing promote physical and mental well-being.

- **Gardening or cooking**: Engaging in hands-on activities fosters mindfulness and provides a break from digital noise.

Strengthening Real-World Relationships

Technology has made communication more convenient, but nothing replaces face-to-face interactions. Investing time in real-world connections can significantly enhance emotional well-being.

- **Schedule in-person meetups**: Prioritize coffee dates, dinners, or outdoor activities with friends and family.

- **Engage in community events**: Volunteering, attending local events, or joining clubs can introduce new social opportunities.

- **Practice deep conversations**: Put away digital distractions when spending time with loved ones to foster meaningful interactions.

The Reward of a Balanced Digital Life

Digital detoxing isn't about rejecting technology altogether but rather about using it in a way that enhances life rather than detracts from it. By taking back control of our attention and time, we can create space for deeper connections, personal growth, and genuine fulfillment. Like Emma's weekend without Wi-Fi, even small breaks from digital distractions can lead to significant improvements in well-being, productivity, and overall happiness. The key is balance, using technology as a tool rather than allowing it to control us.

CHAPTER 7

BUILDING MEANINGFUL FRIENDSHIPS IN A DIGITAL WORLD

An Unexpected Connection

When Nina moved to a new city for work, she found herself feeling incredibly isolated. She barely knew anyone, and her long work hours left her with little opportunity to meet new people in person. One evening, while strolling through an online book club forum, she struck up a conversation with another member, Alex, over their shared love of historical fiction. What began as a simple exchange of book recommendations soon blossomed into daily conversations about life, aspirations, and personal struggles. Months later, when Nina finally met Alex in person at a book festival, she realized something profound: the depth of their friendship, nurtured through digital means, was just as meaningful as any connection she had made offline. But not all online friendships have this level of authenticity. How can we distinguish between genuine digital relationships and fleeting interactions? How do we ensure our friendships, both online and offline, are meaningful and enduring?

The Key Differences Between Online and Offline Friendships

Friendship, at its core, is about trust, support, and emotional connection. However, the medium through which we form and maintain friendships has evolved dramatically with the rise of digital communication. Understanding the differences between online and offline friendships is essential for fostering meaningful relationships in both spaces.

Proximity and Physical Presence

Traditional friendships often grow in environments where people interact regularly, school, workplaces, local clubs, or neighborhoods. These relationships develop naturally through shared experiences, physical gestures, and body language, which strengthen emotional bonds over time. The ability to read facial expressions, hear tonal shifts in conversation, and engage in spontaneous activities all contribute to the richness of offline friendships.

Online friendships, in contrast, lack the immediacy of physical presence. Communication occurs through texts, video calls, or social media interactions, where nonverbal cues can be misinterpreted or absent altogether. While this may pose challenges, it also allows people to connect across great distances and cultural backgrounds, expanding the scope of potential friendships beyond geographical limitations.

Depth of Interaction

Offline friendships typically involve more immersive interactions, from shared meals to participating in hobbies together. These in-person experiences create deep, lasting memories that fortify relationships.

Online friendships often start through shared interests or mutual online communities. While digital connections can become deeply meaningful, they sometimes remain surface-level due to the absence of physical interactions. It's easy to engage in passive communication, liking posts or sending emojis, without truly investing in the relationship. Therefore, making an effort to engage in meaningful conversations is crucial for online friendships to flourish.

Consistency and Commitment

Offline friendships tend to require more effort to maintain, meeting up, traveling to see one another, and setting aside dedicated time. This level of commitment often serves as a testament to the strength of the relationship.

In contrast, online friendships can sometimes feel more disposable. With the ease of sending a message or unfollowing someone, the level of commitment can vary significantly. However, when nurtured properly, digital friendships can be just as strong as offline ones, particularly when both parties show genuine interest and effort in sustaining the connection.

Recognizing Genuine Relationships vs. Shallow Digital Interactions

With social media and instant messaging at our fingertips, it's easy to amass a large network of online acquaintances. However, having hundreds of followers or connections doesn't equate to having meaningful friendships. Identifying genuine relationships in the digital world requires discernment.

Signs of a Genuine Friendship:

1. **Mutual Effort** – Both individuals contribute equally to the conversation and show interest in each other's lives.

2. **Deep Conversations** – Discussions go beyond superficial topics, delving into emotions, aspirations, and vulnerabilities.

3. **Emotional Support** – A true friend is there in times of need, offering encouragement and understanding.

4. **Consistency** – The relationship isn't solely based on sporadic interactions but includes ongoing communication.

5. **Respect and Honesty** – Both parties feel comfortable being authentic and honest without fear of judgment.

Red Flags of a Shallow Digital Connection:

1. **One-Sided Communication** – One person always initiates while the other responds minimally or inconsistently.

2. **Lack of Emotional Depth** – Conversations remain surface-level, focusing only on casual topics like memes or trends.

3. **Transactional Interactions** – The relationship revolves around favors, benefits, or convenience rather than genuine connection.

4. **Ghosting or Ignoring** – Disappearing for long periods or avoiding deeper conversations may indicate a lack of true commitment.

5. **Superficial Validation** – The friendship is based primarily on likes, comments, and online engagement rather than real conversation.

Strengthening Emotional Intelligence for Better Social Connections

Emotional intelligence (EQ) plays a pivotal role in building and maintaining friendships, both online and offline. It involves self-awareness, empathy, and effective communication, all of which contribute to deeper and more fulfilling relationships.

Self-Awareness in Digital Communication

Being mindful of our own emotions and reactions helps us navigate digital friendships more effectively. Recognizing when we're feeling lonely, frustrated, or misunderstood can prevent miscommunication and ensure healthier interactions.

Practicing Empathy Online

Empathy is the ability to understand and share the feelings of another person. In digital interactions, this means:

- Taking the time to listen and respond thoughtfully.
- Avoiding assumptions or misjudging tone in text-based conversations.
- Acknowledging and validating a friend's emotions, even if expressed virtually.

Managing Conflicts in Online Friendships

Disagreements are inevitable in any relationship. In the digital space, conflicts can be exacerbated by the lack of tone and body language. To navigate disputes:

- Address concerns directly and calmly rather than through passive-aggressive posts or ignoring messages.
- Use video or voice calls for serious discussions to prevent misinterpretation.
- Be willing to apologize and make amends when necessary.

Effective Communication Skills for Deep and Lasting Friendships

Strong friendships are built on a foundation of open and honest communication. Developing effective digital communication skills can lead to more meaningful and lasting relationships.

Being Present and Engaged

Just as one wouldn't constantly check their phone during an in-person conversation, it's essential to be fully engaged in online interactions. Responding thoughtfully rather than giving generic replies fosters deeper connections.

Balancing Online and Offline Communication

For those friendships that begin online, finding ways to transition into real-life interactions (when possible) can strengthen the bond. Scheduling video calls, planning meetups, or even sending handwritten letters can add a more personal touch.

Setting Healthy Boundaries

Not all digital interactions are beneficial. Setting boundaries—such as limiting time spent on social media, recognizing toxic relationships, and prioritizing real-life connections, ensures that digital friendships enhance rather than detract from one's well-being.

Expressing Appreciation

A simple message expressing gratitude for a friend's presence in your life can go a long way in deepening the bond. Genuine friendships thrive when both parties feel valued and appreciated.

Conclusion: Nurturing Meaningful Friendships in the Digital Age

As technology continues to shape the way we connect, the challenge lies in ensuring that our digital interactions translate into meaningful and lasting friendships. Whether formed online or offline, genuine relationships require mutual effort, emotional intelligence, and effective communication. By being intentional about the way we build and nurture friendships, we can create connections that not only withstand the digital age but thrive within it.

HANDLING ONLINE DRAMA, TROLLING, AND CYBERBULLYING

The Digital Battlefield: Why Online Conflict Escalates So Quickly

In the vast expanse of the digital world, where billions of people connect daily, conflict is inevitable. Unlike face-to-face interactions, online disputes tend to escalate with astonishing speed. This rapid intensification can be attributed to several factors, including the absence of nonverbal cues, the anonymity afforded by the internet, and the ease with which individuals can misunderstand each other's tone or intent. In digital spaces, people are emboldened to say things they would never articulate in real life, leading to hostile exchanges that spiral out of control.

One major catalyst for online drama is the concept of the **online disinhibition effect**, a psychological phenomenon where individuals feel less accountable for their words and actions in digital spaces. This lack of restraint often results in exaggerated emotions, reactive comments, and impulsive arguments. Additionally, the viral nature of social media enables conflicts to be witnessed, shared, and amplified, transforming a minor disagreement into a full-fledged spectacle. The public nature of online exchanges also invites third-party interventions, further fueling disputes and making resolution increasingly difficult.

To navigate these digital battlegrounds, it's essential to recognize the mechanics of online conflict and the psychological triggers that drive people to engage in digital aggression. Understanding these dynamics can help individuals disengage before becoming ensnared in an unnecessary or destructive online confrontation.

Disengaging from Negativity and Toxic Digital Environments

One of the most effective strategies for handling online drama is learning when and how to disengage. The internet is filled with people who thrive on provoking others, seeking reactions rather than meaningful discussions. Engaging with such individuals only fuels the toxicity, creating an endless cycle of negativity. Recognizing when a conversation has become unproductive or harmful is the first step toward preserving one's peace of mind.

Strategies for Disengagement:

1. **Pause Before Responding:** Take a deep breath before replying to a heated comment. This short pause can prevent knee-jerk reactions that may worsen the situation.

2. **Ask Yourself: Is This Worth My Energy?** Not every battle needs to be fought. If a conversation is unlikely to lead to mutual understanding, it's best to let it go.

3. **Use the Mute or Hide Features:** Many social media platforms allow users to mute conversations or hide comments without outright blocking someone. This is useful when you don't want to escalate the situation but also don't want to see negativity.

4. **Limit Exposure to Toxic Spaces:** If a particular forum or social media group consistently fosters hostility, consider leaving the space or reducing engagement.

5. **Respond with Kindness or Humor:** Sometimes, responding with lightheartedness or kindness can disarm an aggressive person, making it clear that you refuse to engage in negativity.

6. **Know When to Log Off:** Stepping away from the screen can be one of the most powerful ways to reclaim control. Digital spaces

may be chaotic, but they don't have to dominate your emotional well-being.

Protecting Yourself from Cyberbullying and Harassment

Cyberbullying is an unfortunate reality of the internet, affecting people of all ages and backgrounds. Unlike traditional bullying, which is confined to specific locations like school or the workplace, cyberbullying can follow individuals into their homes, making it an ever-present threat. From direct threats and persistent harassment to doxxing (exposing personal information online) and coordinated attacks, the spectrum of online bullying is vast.

Steps to Protect Yourself:

1. **Strengthen Privacy Settings:** Ensure that your social media accounts are set to private, allowing only trusted individuals to view your content.

2. **Avoid Engaging with Aggressors:** Trolls and cyberbullies thrive on reactions. The less attention you give them, the less power they hold over you.

3. **Document Everything:** If you are being harassed online, take screenshots of messages, comments, or posts as evidence in case legal or platform intervention is required.

4. **Report and Block the Offender:** Social media platforms have built-in reporting mechanisms that allow you to flag abusive content. Blocking the individual can also prevent further interactions.

5. **Change Contact Information if Necessary:** If harassment escalates, consider changing your email, username, or phone number to cut off the perpetrator's access to you.

6. **Seek Support:** Confide in friends, family, or professional support groups. Cyberbullying can take a significant emotional toll, and seeking external guidance can help manage its impact.

By proactively safeguarding your online presence, you create barriers that make it more difficult for cyberbullies to affect your digital experience.

The Importance of Digital Resilience and Emotional Detachment

In a world where online interactions are a fundamental part of daily life, developing **digital resilience**, the ability to withstand and recover from negative digital experiences, is crucial. Emotional detachment, in this context, does not mean indifference but rather maintaining a level-headed approach to online interactions.

Building Digital Resilience:

1. **Recognize That Online Words Hold Only the Power You Give Them:** Not every negative comment deserves your attention or validation.

2. **Practice Emotional Regulation:** If a comment or message upsets you, step away from the screen, take a walk, or practice mindfulness before deciding on a response.

3. **Develop a Support System:** Surround yourself with positive digital communities and trusted friends who uplift and support you.

4. **Engage in Offline Activities:** The more balanced your life is between online and offline interactions; the less impact digital negativity will have on you.

5. **Adopt a Growth Mindset:** Understand that facing online challenges can help build emotional strength. Instead of seeing cyberbullying as a defining moment, view it as an opportunity to reinforce your resilience.

By cultivating these habits, you strengthen your ability to navigate digital spaces without being consumed by negativity.

How to Report, Block, and Move on from Online Negativity

Despite our best efforts, encountering online hostility is sometimes unavoidable. Knowing how to take swift action against cyberbullying, trolling, and harassment ensures that these experiences don't linger longer than necessary.

Reporting Abuse:

Most social media platforms and websites have dedicated reporting mechanisms to handle abuse. Familiarize yourself with these tools so you can act promptly:

- **Facebook & Instagram:** Report posts, comments, messages, or accounts through their 'Report' feature.
- **Twitter/X:** Use the 'Report Tweet' or 'Block and Report' functions for abusive content.
- **YouTube:** Flag inappropriate videos or comments.
- **Reddit:** Use the report feature to alert moderators about rule-breaking content.
- **Gaming Platforms:** Most online gaming services, including Xbox Live, PlayStation Network, and Steam, have reporting features for toxic behavior.

Blocking Aggressors:

If someone persistently harasses you, blocking them is a simple yet powerful move. Once blocked, they cannot interact with you, and their messages or comments will no longer be visible to you. Some platforms also offer 'restrict' options, allowing you to limit a person's engagement without notifying them.

Moving On:

Once an incident is dealt with, focus on moving forward. Constantly revisiting negative interactions can take a toll on mental health. Instead, redirect your energy to positive engagements, hobbies, or meaningful conversations. Remember, online negativity is a temporary disruption, but your well-being is a long-term priority.

Final Thoughts: Reclaiming Control in the Digital World

The internet can be a beautiful space for learning, connection, and creativity, but it also has its dark corners. Understanding the mechanics of online conflict, developing disengagement strategies, protecting yourself from cyberbullying, and building emotional resilience are crucial steps in maintaining a healthy digital presence.

By taking control of your online experiences, you ensure that the negativity of the digital world does not overshadow the vast opportunities it offers. The internet should be a tool that enhances your life, not a space where you feel drained, anxious, or unsafe. Stay mindful, stay empowered, and most importantly, remember that you have the power to curate your digital environment.

CHAPTER 9

SOCIAL MEDIA FOR GOOD: USING PLATFORMS WITH PURPOSE

The Ripple Effect of a Single Post

Mia had always enjoyed scrolling through social media, but she never imagined that one post could change her life. It all started with a simple act of sharing, a heartfelt story about her struggles with anxiety and how she found solace in journaling. She posted it on a whim, unsure if anyone would even read it. The next morning, she woke up to an avalanche of comments and messages from people who resonated with her experience. Strangers thanked her for her vulnerability, saying her words gave them comfort and the courage to share their own stories. That moment reshaped her perspective on social media; it wasn't just about entertainment or distraction; it was a powerful tool for connection, growth, and positive impact.

How to Cultivate a Healthy Relationship with Social Media

Social media, like any tool, can be used constructively or destructively. The key lies in fostering a healthy relationship with it. This begins with self-awareness, understanding why you engage with social media and how it affects your emotions and mental well-being.

One effective approach is setting boundaries. Establish screen time limits, take regular digital detoxes, and be mindful of the content you consume. Curate your feed intentionally, following accounts that inspire, educate, or bring joy rather than those that trigger comparison or negativity.

Another important aspect is engaging mindfully. Instead of aimless scrolling, approach social media with purpose. Use it as a means to learn, grow, and connect meaningfully with others. Participate in discussions that challenge your thinking, share content that adds value, and be deliberate about the messages you put out into the world.

Leveraging Online Platforms for Personal Growth and Career Opportunities

Beyond entertainment and social interaction, social media is a goldmine for personal and professional development. Platforms like LinkedIn, Twitter, and Instagram have paved the way for individuals to showcase their skills, build personal brands, and connect with opportunities they might never have encountered otherwise.

To maximize social media for career growth, start by optimizing your profile. Whether it's a LinkedIn resume, an Instagram portfolio, or a YouTube channel, your digital presence should reflect your expertise and aspirations. Share industry insights, engage with professionals in your field, and use strategic hashtags to increase visibility.

Additionally, learning is at your fingertips. Many influencers and industry leaders share valuable knowledge through tweets, podcasts, and live sessions. Engaging with this content can expand your skillset and keep you updated on trends relevant to your field.

The Power of Digital Advocacy and Creating Positive Impact

Social media has become a catalyst for change, empowering individuals to raise awareness about social causes, mobilize communities, and drive action. From climate activism to mental health awareness, digital advocacy has proven its ability to amplify voices and inspire global movements.

To be an effective digital advocate, focus on authenticity. Share causes that truly matter to you and back them up with credible sources. Engage in meaningful conversations rather than performative activism, take real action beyond social media, such as volunteering, donating, or educating others in your local community.

Micro-activism also plays a role in positive impact. Even small acts, such as resharing a petition, promoting a small business, or offering words of encouragement to someone in need, contribute to creating a more compassionate and informed online space.

How to Curate a Mindful and Inspiring Social Media Presence

Your online presence should reflect your values and aspirations while fostering a community of like-minded individuals. Start by defining your purpose, what do you want your social media to represent? Whether it's creativity, motivation, humor, or education, staying true to this vision will attract a more engaged and supportive audience.

Consistency is key. While you don't have to post daily, having a consistent theme or message helps establish your identity. High-quality content, whether through visuals, storytelling, or educational posts, adds value to your followers' experience.

Additionally, engage with your audience in a genuine way. Respond to comments, participate in discussions, and support fellow creators. A mindful and inspiring presence isn't just about the content you post; it's about the community you nurture.

Becoming a Role Model for Responsible and Conscious Social Media Use

In an era where misinformation, cyberbullying, and unrealistic portrayals of life are rampant, being a role model for ethical social media use is more important than ever. Leading by example means practicing digital etiquette, fact-checking before sharing, crediting original creators, and being mindful of the language you use online.

Encourage positive interactions by promoting kindness and inclusivity. Call out harmful behavior when necessary but do so constructively. If you have a platform, use it responsibly support important causes, amplify marginalized voices, and create a safe space for open discussions.

Teaching younger generations how to navigate social media is also crucial. If you have siblings, mentees, or children in your life, guide them on responsible digital behavior, privacy settings, and the importance of a healthy balance between online and offline activities.

Final Thoughts: Shaping the Future of Social Media for Good

Social media is a reflection of how we choose to use it. When approached with mindfulness, purpose, and integrity, it becomes a force for connection, education, and empowerment. Each post, comment, and interaction contribute to the larger online ecosystem, so why not make it one that uplifts and inspires?

Mia's story is a testament to the ripple effect that even a single post can have. Just as she transformed her social media experience into one of healing and advocacy, each of us has the power to use our digital presence to make a difference. Whether it's through storytelling, supporting a cause, or simply spreading positivity, let's ensure that the time we spend online is meaningful, impactful, and rooted in purpose.

THE FUTURE OF SOCIAL SAVVINESS: LIFELONG SKILLS FOR CONFIDENCE AND SUCCESS

The Elevator Ride That Changed Everything

A few years ago, a young entrepreneur named Priscilia found herself in an elevator with a high-profile investor she had long admired. It was the perfect opportunity to make an impression, but nerves got the best of her. She stumbled over her words, failing to convey her business vision confidently. As the doors opened and the investor stepped out, Priscilia realized she had missed a golden chance. That moment stayed with her, not as a failure but as a lesson, being socially savvy isn't just about making connections; it's about seizing opportunities with confidence, emotional intelligence, and adaptability.

Priscilia committed herself to developing her social skills, ensuring that the next time she found herself in such a moment, she would be prepared. Years later, at a networking event, she met the same investor. This time, her conversation was fluid, engaging, and confident. The investor not only remembered her but also showed keen interest in her business. This transformation was the result of years of social awareness, adaptability, and self-improvement, skills that anyone can cultivate for long-term success.

How Social Awareness Translates to Long-Term Personal and Professional Success

Social awareness is more than a soft skill; it is a strategic advantage in both personal and professional life. Individuals who cultivate social savviness tend to navigate relationships, workplaces, and networking environments with ease. The ability to read a room, adapt communication styles, and engage in meaningful conversations opens doors that might otherwise remain closed.

Professionally, social awareness helps build strong networks, create collaborative teams, and foster a positive reputation. Leaders who understand their colleagues' emotions and motivations inspire loyalty and productivity. Employees with high social intelligence stand out in interviews, negotiate better salaries, and thrive in the workplace dynamics.

On a personal level, social savviness enhances relationships by fostering empathy, understanding, and connection. It strengthens friendships, improves conflict resolution, and builds emotional resilience. Those who master social awareness tend to have richer, more fulfilling lives because they know how to engage meaningfully with others.

Success is rarely achieved in isolation. Whether advancing in a career or maintaining fulfilling personal relationships, the ability to interact effectively with others is invaluable. The key is recognizing that social skills are not innate; they can be learned, refined, and mastered over time.

Developing Adaptability in an Ever-Changing Digital and Social Landscape

The rapid evolution of technology and communication platforms requires constant adaptation. The way people interact today is vastly different from how they did even a decade ago. Social norms shift, digital etiquette evolves, and the ability to keep up determines one's social effectiveness.

Adaptability means understanding different communication channels, from face-to-face conversations to virtual meetings and social media interactions. Each platform demands a unique approach. For example, what works in a professional LinkedIn post may not be suitable for an informal Twitter exchange.

One major challenge in the digital age is maintaining authenticity while adapting to new social trends. Many people struggle with presenting a polished yet genuine versions of themselves online. Successful individuals strike a balance by maintaining a consistent voice while being flexible enough to embrace new communication styles.

Adaptability also involves handling criticism and feedback gracefully. The digital space exposes individuals to diverse opinions, sometimes leading to conflict or misunderstandings. Those who can navigate these challenges with composure and a growth mindset emerge stronger and more socially adept.

To stay ahead, individuals must continuously refine their digital and interpersonal communication skills. This may involve taking online courses, observing industry trends, and engaging in meaningful discussions both online and offline. Social adaptability is not about changing who you are; it is about evolving with the world while maintaining your core values.

The Importance of Self-Awareness and Emotional Intelligence in Future Interactions

Self-awareness is the cornerstone of social effectiveness. It involves understanding one's strengths, weaknesses, emotions, and triggers. When individuals know themselves well, they can engage with others in a more conscious and intentional way.

Emotional intelligence (EI) goes hand in hand with self-awareness. It includes recognizing emotions in oneself and others, managing interpersonal relationships judiciously, and responding to situations with empathy and control. High EI individuals tend to build stronger networks, resolve conflicts effectively, and handle stress with resilience.

In future social interactions, emotional intelligence will be even more critical. As automation and artificial intelligence become more integrated into daily life, the human touch will be a differentiator. Empathy, active listening, and genuine connection will set individuals apart in both professional and personal realms.

Developing self-awareness and emotional intelligence requires ongoing reflection and practice. Mindfulness exercises, journaling, and seeking constructive feedback are effective ways to enhance these skills. The better individuals understand themselves, the more effectively they can connect with others.

Setting Personal Goals for Ongoing Social Growth and Digital Well-Being

Mastering social savviness is not a one-time achievement; it is a lifelong pursuit. Setting personal goals for social growth ensures continuous improvement and adaptability. These goals can range from improving conversational skills to becoming more comfortable in networking settings.

One approach is to establish specific, measurable goals. For instance:

- **Enhancing networking skills:** Attend at least one networking event per month and engage in meaningful conversations.

- **Improving digital communication:** Learn how to craft more engaging and professional emails or social media posts.

- **Strengthening emotional intelligence:** Practice active listening by summarizing what others say before responding.

- **Expanding cultural awareness:** Read books or take courses on different cultural communication styles to improve global interactions.

Digital well-being is another essential aspect of social growth. Setting boundaries for screen time, curating positive online interactions, and taking breaks from social media contribute to a healthier digital life. Social connectivity should enhance well-being, not diminish it.

By setting personal goals and revisiting them regularly, individuals ensure they remain socially adept and confident in all interactions.

Final Thoughts on Embracing a Socially Savvy Mindset for Life

Social savviness is not a skill that one learns once and forgets; it is a mindset that must be cultivated throughout life. The ability to communicate effectively, adapt to change, and understand others will always be valuable.

Lisa's story from the beginning of this chapter illustrates the importance of continuous social growth. What once seemed like an intimidating skill became her greatest asset. Her journey shows that anyone can develop confidence and social awareness with dedication and practice.

In a world that is becoming increasingly interconnected yet digitally fragmented, those who master social intelligence will thrive. The future belongs to those who embrace adaptability, emotional intelligence, and lifelong learning. Social savviness is not just about impressing others; it is about creating meaningful connections, seizing opportunities, and living a confident and fulfilling life.

As you move forward, challenge yourself to engage more deeply in conversations, step out of your comfort zone, and embrace the evolving social landscape. The skills you cultivate today will shape your success for years to come.

CHAPTER 11

WHO ARE YOU, REALLY? DISCOVERING YOUR AUTHENTIC SELF

Section 1: The Mask We Wear

Have you ever caught yourself smiling when you didn't want to, agreeing with something that didn't sit right with you, or dressing a certain way just to blend in? If so, welcome to the club; it's called being human. From a young age, we learn to wear masks. Not literal ones (unless you're into costume parties), but the invisible kind: polite, agreeable, curated versions of ourselves that help us "fit in."

In today's world, especially with social media acting like a 24/7 spotlight, it's easy to get caught in a cycle of performance. Carefully edited photos, captions that sound profound but don't reflect real emotions, and that constant pressure to appear as though we have it all together; it's exhausting. We edit our lives down to highlight reels, forgetting that real life includes bloopers.

Social Media: The Stage of Perfection

Let's be honest: most of us aren't showing our messy rooms, failed tests, or ugly-cry faces on Instagram. We present our best selves, filtered, curated, and strategically captioned. While there's nothing wrong with wanting to share good moments, the danger lies in mistaking the performance for the person.

This performative culture can nudge us away from authenticity. We start asking, "What will people think?" instead of "What feels right to me?" Likes become validation, and over time, we lose touch with who we really are when no one is watching.

Peer Pressure & Cultural Norms: The Quiet Sculptors

Social norms whisper rules about how to act, what to wear, who to date, and even what career to pursue. Add to that peer pressure, the not-so-subtle nudges from friends or family, and you've got a recipe for identity confusion. It's not always malicious. Sometimes, it's well-meaning people projecting their fears or unfulfilled dreams onto us.

Fitting in becomes the goal. But let's pause and unpack that.

The Difference Between Fitting In and Belonging

Brené Brown, a researcher known for her work on vulnerability and authenticity, offers a beautiful distinction: *Fitting in is about becoming who you need to be to be accepted. Belonging is about being accepted for who you already are.*

Fitting in requires shapeshifting. Belonging invites you to be whole. And there's a huge emotional cost to all that shapeshifting, one that shows up in ways we'll explore later.

But first, let's talk about what happens when you stop performing and start embracing who you really are.

Section 2: Why Authenticity Matters

If being yourself sounds like a cheesy Instagram quote or a throwaway line from a Disney movie, let's give it the weight it deserves. Authenticity isn't just about "being real." It's about living in alignment with your values, desires, and identity; even when it's hard. Especially when it's hard.

So, why does it matter?

The Psychological Benefits

Living authentically leads to lower levels of anxiety, depression, and stress. When you're constantly pretending or censoring yourself, your brain registers that as danger; it's like living in a constant state of low-level threat. But when you show up as yourself, your nervous system relaxes. You're not acting anymore. You're simply being.

The Emotional Benefits

Authenticity breeds self-trust. Every time you honor your truth, whether it's saying no, setting a boundary, or sharing your real opinion, you tell yourself, *I've got your back*. That kind of internal loyalty builds confidence and resilience over time.

The Social Benefits

Here's the ironic twist: the more you embrace your quirks, passions, and truths, the more you attract people who *actually* get you. You stop collecting shallow friendships built on performance and start forming deep connections rooted in realness.

Real Stories: Young Adults Who Dared to Be Different

- **Jasmine**, 23, left a high-paying tech job to start a small eco-business because she couldn't shake the feeling she was living someone else's dream. "Everyone thought I was crazy," she said. "But for the first time, I felt free."

- **Chris**, 19, came out as non-binary after years of hiding behind gender norms. "I lost some people. But I found myself. And that was worth everything."

- **Ravi**, 26, chose to pursue music over medicine, despite family expectations. "My parents were disappointed. But now, they see how alive I am when I perform."

These aren't just feel-good stories, they're evidence that stepping into authenticity, though risky, often leads to a deeper sense of peace and purpose.

Section 3: Signs You're Not Being True to Yourself

Let's get real. You might think everything's fine on the outside, but your body and emotions often give subtle clues when something's off. If you've been living out of sync with your authentic self, you might recognize some of these signs:

1. Chronic Anxiety and Burnout

When you're constantly trying to please everyone, hold up a persona, or chase an identity that isn't yours, it's like running a marathon in someone else's shoes, uncomfortable, painful, and unsustainable. Anxiety becomes a background noise you can't mute. Burnout feels like you're emotionally flatlining.

2. Social Fatigue

You might notice that after socializing, you feel more drained than energized. That's often a sign you're masking, consciously or unconsciously shifting your behavior to suit others. Authentic social interactions should fill your cup, not empty it.

3. The "Chameleon" Syndrome

Do you change your opinions, style, or interests depending on who you're with? That's the classic chameleon move. It's often born out of a fear of rejection, but it also leads to an identity crisis. If you're constantly adapting, you never get the chance to find out what truly resonates with *you*.

4. Feeling Like an Impostor in Your Own Life

This one's deep. You might be successful on paper, surrounded by people, seemingly thriving. And yet, there's a gnawing emptiness, a voice whispering, "This isn't who you are." That disconnect is the soul's call to return home.

So how do you begin that return?

Section 4: Finding Your Voice

Finding your authentic self isn't a one-time epiphany; it's a practice. Like tuning a radio, it takes patience, trial and error, and a lot of quieting the noise around you. Here are some tools to help you find your frequency:

Journaling Prompts to Get You Started

1. When do I feel most *me*?

2. What am I pretending to like that I actually don't?

3. What would I do if I weren't afraid of judgment?

4. What values matter most to me, and where am I living out of alignment with them?

5. Who am I when no one is watching?

Identify Your Strengths

Use tools like the VIA Character Strengths Survey or StrengthsFinder. But also ask friends and family: *What do you think my superpower is?* You'll often be surprised by how others see you.

Discover Your Values

Make a list of 20 values (e.g., freedom, kindness, loyalty, creativity), then narrow it down to your top five. These are your compass. If a decision doesn't align with them, it's probably not for you.

Follow Your Curiosity

Passion is a loud word, but curiosity is softer—and often more sustainable. What topics, activities, or causes naturally pull your attention? Follow that thread.

Explore Your Purpose

Don't stress about having a grand "life mission." Start small. Ask: *How can I contribute to the world in a way that feels meaningful to me?* Purpose evolves. The key is staying connected to what feels real.

Section 5: Creating Your Identity Roadmap

So, how do you put all this into action? Think of this section as your personal GPS, a way to track where you've been, where you are, and where you're going.

Step 1: Reflect on the Past

Write a "personal timeline" highlighting defining moments in your life, both good and hard. These moments often reveal patterns, lessons, and shifts in identity.

Questions to consider:

- What stories have shaped me?
- What messages about identity did I absorb from family, school, or culture?
- Which parts of my past am I still carrying that no longer serve me?

Step 2: Take an Honest Inventory of the Present

Create three lists:

- What energizes me?
- What drains me?
- What do I pretend to like because I think I "should"?

This exercise helps filter out the noise and spotlight where your energy naturally flows.

Step 3: Envision the Future

Picture the most authentic version of yourself in five years. Don't worry about being realistic, go for *resonant*. Ask:

- What does my day look like?
- Who am I surrounded by?
- How do I feel in my own skin?

- What am I creating, contributing, or learning?

Write it all down. Draw it. Create a vision board. Make it vivid.

Step 4: Set Identity Goals

These aren't traditional "achievement" goals, they're about becoming. Examples:

- Speak up in group settings at least once a week.

- Start a blog to share your honest thoughts.

- Say no to things that don't align with your values.

Each action, no matter how small, is a vote for the person you want to be.

Step 5: Revisit and Revise

Authenticity isn't a static endpoint; it's a living, evolving process. Check in every few months:

- Am I moving closer to the life that feels like mine?

- Where am I still people-pleasing or performing?

- What needs to shift?

You don't need to have it all figured out. You just need to keep coming home to yourself.

Final Thoughts: The Permission Slip You've Been Waiting For

Here's your permission slip to stop performing. To be weird, wild, quiet, bold, messy, evolving, unsure. To change your mind. To say, "I don't know who I am right now, but I'm figuring it out."

Your authentic self isn't something you *find*; it's something you *remember*. It's who you were before the world told you who to be. And every small step toward that truth is a revolution.

So go ahead; drop the mask. The world needs the real you.

CHAPTER 12

SHOWING UP REAL, NAVIGATING SOCIAL SPACES WITH CONFIDENCE

1. Social Survival vs. Social Thriving

In every social interaction, we bring not just our presence, but a lifetime of internal narratives, insecurities, learned behaviors, and hopes. Many of us navigate the world with a subtle (or not-so-subtle) sense of caution, measuring how much of ourselves we can show, how loudly we can laugh, or how directly we can speak. This is **social survival**, and while it may help you avoid conflict, it doesn't build deep connection or self-respect.

Thriving socially means more than just having friends or being invited places; it means bringing your full self into every room and knowing you're enough. It's about shifting from "Will they like me?" to "Do I enjoy being here?"

The Psychology Behind Shrinking

Shrinking in social spaces often stems from internalized beliefs picked up in childhood or adolescence, maybe you were told to be "polite," to not interrupt, to "not make a scene." Maybe you learned that being too loud, too opinionated, or too different made you a target. These survival instincts are valid, but they're also outdated in adult spaces where authenticity is the new currency of connection.

Ask yourself: **In which rooms do you hide parts of yourself to fit in?** That answer is your starting point.

The Trap of Overperforming

On the other end of the spectrum lies **overperformance**, being the entertainer, the caretaker, the peacemaker, or the perfectionist. It's exhausting, and worse, it sets the tone for one-sided relationships.

You might overperform if:

- You leave conversations feeling emotionally drained
- You laugh at jokes that aren't funny just to avoid awkwardness
- You constantly manage other people's comfort at the expense of your own

Here's the truth: you don't need to audition for belonging. You already qualify.

How to Transition from Survival to Thriving

1. Rehearse Realness

Practice saying what you actually think, in small, low-stakes situations at first. Say "I don't agree" or "That's not really my thing" and see what happens. Most times, the world won't fall apart.

2. Set an Inner Anchor

Before entering a social situation, take a breath and remind yourself: "I am enough. I don't need to perform to belong."

3. Evaluate the Room

Sometimes we blame ourselves for discomfort when really, we're just in the wrong room. Being real isn't about fitting in everywhere; it's about knowing where you naturally thrive.

2. Owning Your Space Without Apology

Confidence isn't about being the loudest voice in the room; it's about being at peace with your voice, no matter the volume. Owning your space means you move through the world knowing your presence is valid, not up for negotiation, not contingent on approval.

The Power of Speaking Up

Many women have been conditioned to defer, deflect, or dilute their thoughts to avoid conflict. But self-expression is not aggression. Speaking clearly about your needs and opinions isn't rude; it's respectful to both yourself and others.

Scripts for Speaking Up:

- "Actually, I see it a bit differently…"

- "Thanks for sharing your perspective here's mine…"

- "I'm not comfortable with that, and I'd appreciate if we could change the subject."

Boundary-Setting as a Skill

Boundaries aren't walls; they're **clarity**. They tell people where you begin and where you end. And guess what? The people who truly value you will respect your boundaries. The ones who don't? They benefit from your lack of them.

Boundary Script Starters:

- "That doesn't work for me."

- "I need a bit of space right now."

- "Let's revisit this when I've had time to think."

Body Language and Energy

Even before we speak, we communicate. Owning your space also means using your body and presence with intention.

Posture matters. Shoulders back, chin level, feet grounded. You deserve to take up physical space.

Eye contact. It signals engagement, not confrontation.

Stillness. Fidgeting or nervous laughter can signal discomfort. Take a deep breath and center yourself.

Navigating Awkward Moments

Awkward moments aren't social failures, they're just human glitches. Handle them with grace and humor.

Example: You forget someone's name mid-conversation. Try: "I'm so sorry, remind me your name again. I want to get it right."

You say something that lands wrong. Try: "Hmm, that came out weird. Let me rephrase."

The goal isn't perfection; it's connection.

3. The Power of "No" and "I'm Not Okay"

Too often, women are taught to be agreeable, accommodating, and emotionally available at all times. But **your "no" is powerful.** It protects your time, your energy, and your peace. And so is your "I'm not okay." It invites compassion and connection, not pity or weakness.

Emotional Boundaries 101

Emotional boundaries mean you are not responsible for managing other people's emotions or suppressing your own to make them comfortable.

Healthy emotional boundaries sound like:

- "I can listen, but I can't take this on right now."
- "I understand you're upset, but it's not okay to speak to me that way."
- "I need some time to process this before continuing the conversation."

Practicing the Power of "No"

"No" doesn't have to be followed by an essay or an apology.

Ways to say no with confidence:

- "Thanks for thinking of me, but I'll pass."

- "I'm not available for that right now."
- "No, but I hope it goes well!"

Saying no is like a muscle; it gets stronger with use.

Vulnerability: A Bridge, not a Breakdown

Saying "I'm not okay" in trusted spaces is an act of courage. It allows for deeper human connection and builds emotional intimacy. You don't have to be the strong one all the time.

Try saying:

- "Today's been hard. I could use a friend."
- "I'm going through something right now and feeling overwhelmed."
- "I'm struggling, and I don't need solutions, just a safe space."

The right people will lean in, not run away.

4. Finding Your People

Let's get real: not everyone who smiles at you is your friend. Not everyone who cheers for you in public supports you in private. **Finding your people is not about quantity; it's about quality.**

Spotting the Real from the Fake

Real friends:

- Celebrate your wins without comparison
- Call you out with love, not judgment
- Respect your boundaries and value your voice

Fake friends:

- Disappear when you need them most
- Only show up when it benefits them
- Subtly compete or undermine you

Red Flags:

- Passive-aggressive comments
- One-sided conversations
- Chronic flakiness or emotional unavailability

The Beauty of Small Circles

You don't need a crowd; you need a **crew**. A few people who get you, love you as you are, and show up when it counts.

Big vibes, small circle. That's the magic formula.

Ask yourself:

- Who do I feel lighter around?
- Who can I be messy and real with?
- Who claps for me even when they're struggling?

Those are your people.

How to Cultivate Genuine Connection

1. Be curious, not performative.

Ask meaningful questions. Listen fully. People know when you're present vs. polite.

2. Share intentionally.

Vulnerability invites vulnerability. But lead with discernment.

3. Follow up.

A simple "How did that thing go?" text shows you care.

Connection takes effort, but it also pays in soul currency.

4. Authenticity in the Digital Age

We now live in a world where it's easier to perform than to be. Online spaces often reward perfection, controversy, or curated chaos. But **authenticity still matters**, maybe now more than ever.

Being Real Without Oversharing

There's a difference between vulnerability and emotional dumping. You don't owe the internet your breakdowns to prove you're "real."

Ask yourself:

- Am I sharing to connect or to be validated?
- Have I processed this experience enough to share it responsibly?
- Would I be okay if this didn't get a lot of likes?

Boundaries online look like:

- Not responding to every DM
- Not explaining your choices
- Taking breaks when it gets too noisy

Digital Detox and Self-Worth

Your worth is not tied to your follower count, engagement rate, or who views your stories. Likes are not love. And validation is fleeting if it's not rooted inside.

Try this challenge:

Go one day without social media. Notice what thoughts come up. Are you bored? Anxious? Relieved?

Now try this:

- Turn off notifications for 24 hours.
- Remove one app that drains you.
- Replace scrolling with something that restores you, a walk, journaling, calling a friend.

Reclaim your mental real estate.

Curating vs. Faking

It's okay to curate your online presence, but not at the expense of your truth.

Tips for staying grounded:

- Follow people who inspire, not trigger you
- Mute or unfollow accounts that feed comparison
- Post what you love, not what performs

Your online life should reflect you, not a version of you optimized for applause.

Final Thoughts: Real Is Revolutionary

In a world that often pressures us to be agreeable, aesthetic, and endlessly available, **showing up real is a quiet rebellion**. It's a declaration that you trust your voice, your values, and your vibe, even if not everyone else does.

When you stop performing and start presenting your authentic self, you shift the energy in every room you enter. You attract deeper friendships, make more confident choices, and find peace that's not dependent on external validation.

So, walk into every space knowing this:

You don't have to shrink to be loved.

You don't have to shout to be heard.

You just have to show up real.

CHAPTER 13

GROWING BOLD, BUILDING A FUTURE AROUND THE REAL YOU

Section 1: What Growth Really Looks Like

Let's be real, growth doesn't come with a glamorous highlight reel. It's messy, nonlinear, often uncomfortable, and rarely comes with applause. But if you're waiting for some magical moment when everything aligns and you're suddenly the best version of yourself, stop. Growth isn't a lightning bolt. It's a slow burn.

Progress Over Perfection

The first rule of growing into your real self is ditching the illusion of perfection. Perfection is a performance. Progress, on the other hand, is truth. It's the awkward attempts, the course corrections, the wins no one sees, and the courage to keep showing up.

Think about a baby learning to walk. They fall, laugh, cry, and try again. No one expects them to nail it on the first go, so why do we expect that of ourselves in adulthood? Real growth looks like choosing to get back up one more time. It's being kind to yourself when you fail and choosing to learn instead of loathe.

Embracing Mistakes as Part of the Journey

Mistakes aren't signs you're on the wrong path; they're proof you're moving. Every error is a breadcrumb toward insight. When you bomb a presentation, get ghosted by a friend, or make a career misstep, ask yourself: What did this teach me about myself? About what I value? About how I want to live?

Your journey will be full of "what was I thinking?" moments. That's good. It means you're alive and learning. Growth is less about being right and more about being real. It's not linear; it loops, spirals, and sometimes stalls. But even when you feel stuck, you're building resilience. That's growth, too.

Section 2: Choosing Role Models (Not Just Influencers)

We live in an age of influence, where likes and follows can feel like credibility. But being popular online isn't the same as being wise in real life. So let's get clear: a role model isn't someone with a curated feed. It's someone who lives with integrity, even when no one's watching.

How to Find Mentors, Online or Offline

A mentor isn't always someone with a fancy title or ten years on you. They can be your colleague, your neighbor, your coach, or even someone you've never met but admire deeply. Look for those who've walked a path that resonates with your goals and values.

Mentors don't always come to you. Sometimes, you have to initiate the connection. Reach out. Ask questions. Express genuine interest. People are often more willing to share their wisdom than you think. And if you're seeking inspiration online, look beyond the aesthetic. Look for people who share their struggles as well as their successes. Vulnerability is the new credibility.

What to Look for in a Person Worth Following

Not every loud voice is a wise one. Seek out people who embody qualities you want to build in yourself, courage, consistency, empathy, authenticity. Are they growing, or just performing? Do they uplift others or only talk about themselves? Are they rooted in purpose or popularity?

The best mentors don't just teach you; they challenge you. They call you out when you're playing small. They encourage you to think for yourself, not become a clone of them. And they live what they preach, even when it's inconvenient.

Surround yourself with people whose energy stretches you, not drains you. You don't need a cheerleader for your ego. You need a mirror for your soul.

Section 3: Designing Your Environment for Growth

You can't plant a seed in concrete and expect it to flourish. In the same way, your environment has a massive impact on how authentically you can grow. Growth isn't just about mindset; it's about your setup.

Routines, Habits, and Support Systems That Reinforce Authenticity

Want to know what shapes your future? The little things you do daily. Morning routines, evening wind-downs, time to reflect, space to dream, these aren't luxuries. They're tools.

Design rituals that ground you in who you are. Maybe it's journaling each morning, walking in silence, checking in weekly with a growth-minded friend, or scheduling a "real talk" session with yourself every Sunday. When your routine reflects your values, your life begins to, too.

Create accountability with people who get it. Build micro-communities around growth, group chats, book clubs, masterminds, or even just one trusted person you can text when you're spiraling. You don't have to do this alone.

Managing Triggers and Avoiding Toxic Environments

Let's talk about the environments that suffocate growth. The comparison vortex of social media. The draining friend who dismisses your dreams. The job that values your silence over your voice. These spaces can shrink your sense of self.

Start identifying your personal triggers. What makes you question your worth? What patterns cause you to shut down or self-sabotage?

Awareness is power. Once you know what dims your light, you can start to make changes.

Set boundaries like your life depends on it because it does. Limit your exposure to people, places, and platforms that pull you away from your real self. Create sacred spaces, digital and physical, where you can breathe, create, and reset.

You don't need a perfect environment, just an intentional one. The goal isn't to eliminate discomfort but to surround yourself with enough safety to take brave steps.

Section 4: Making Your Own Chance in Life

Waiting for the "right time" is a trap. Life rarely hands us golden tickets. Most of the time, you have to make your own luck, and that means getting uncomfortable.

Saying Yes to Opportunities Even When You're Scared

Growth starts where comfort ends. Saying yes when you're scared is like telling your future self, "I believe in you, even if I don't fully see you yet."

That might mean applying for the job you don't feel 100% qualified for. Speaking up in the meeting even though your voice shakes. Trying something new and letting yourself be a beginner.

Fear is a signal that something matters. Instead of avoiding it, lean into it. Every brave "yes" is a muscle-builder for self-trust. And self-trust? That's your ticket to real freedom.

Turning Rejection and Setbacks into Power

You will be told no. You will mess up. You will feel like you're not enough at times. This is not a sign to stop; it's your signal to dig deeper.

Rejection is not redirection. Sometimes it's protection. Sometimes it's preparation. And sometimes, it's just a plot twist on your timeline.

Don't internalize rejection as failure. Use it as fuel. Journal what you learned. Reflect on what you'd do differently. Then get back in the ring.

Every "no" can sharpen your clarity. Every closed door can push you toward one you wouldn't have knocked on otherwise. The people who grow bold don't wait for ideal conditions. They build in the middle of chaos.

Section 5: Your Next Chapter Starts Now

This isn't a theory. It's a practice. It's not about knowing; it's about doing. You've done the reflection. Now it's time to live it.

Creating a Personal Mission Statement

A personal mission statement is like a compass for your future. It keeps you grounded in your "why" when life gets noisy. It can be a sentence, a mantra, or a short paragraph that encapsulates who you are and what you stand for.

Ask yourself:

- What matters most to me?
- How do I want to show up in the world?
- What impact do I want to have?
- What values do I want to guide my actions?

Here's a sample to inspire you:

"I am committed to living boldly, choosing truth over comfort, and using my voice to create space for others to do the same."

Make it yours. Write it, speak it, and revisit it often. Your mission isn't fixed; it can evolve as you do.

21-Day Authenticity Challenge

Here's your chance to put everything into practice. For the next 21 days, commit to one action daily that aligns with the real you. Here's a sample roadmap to get you started:

Week 1 – Self-Discovery

- Day 1: Write a letter to your younger self.
- Day 2: Identify 3 core values and why they matter.
- Day 3: Unfollow accounts that trigger insecurity.
- Day 4: Reflect on a past mistake and what it taught you.
- Day 5: Spend 30 minutes alone, no phone, no distraction.
- Day 6: Name one fear that's holding you back.
- Day 7: Do something creative without judging the result.

Week 2 – Bold Expression

- Day 8: Say something you've been holding back (with kindness).
- Day 9: Try something new and uncomfortable.
- Day 10: Post or share something true to you, not curated.
- Day 11: Set one boundary you've been avoiding.
- Day 12: Revisit your mission statement.
- Day 13: Ask someone for honest feedback.
- Day 14: Wear something that makes you feel powerful.

Week 3 – Future Building

- Day 15: List your top 3 long-term goals.
- Day 16: Research someone doing what you dream of.
- Day 17: Take one step toward a scary but exciting goal.
- Day 18: Journal where you want to be in 5 years.
- Day 19: Create a vision board (digital or physical).

- Day 20: Have a "next chapter" conversation with someone who gets it.

- Day 21: Celebrate your boldest moment from the last 3 weeks.

You don't have to be fearless, just willing. Growth doesn't demand perfection. It asks for presence. And when you live in alignment with the real you, you stop chasing a version of yourself and start becoming her.

Final Thoughts: Becoming Is a Bold Act

Growing bold isn't about becoming someone else; it's about peeling back the layers to return to who you've always been underneath the noise. The future isn't something you wait for. It's something you build, brick by brick, decision by decision.

You already have what it takes. The tools, the truth, the fire. Now, the question is: What will you do with it?

Start now. Start messy. But most importantly, start as *you*.

CHAPTER 14

KNOWING YOURSELF FIRST: THE FOUNDATION OF HEALTHY SOCIAL LIFE

Have you ever found yourself struggling to understand who you truly are? Many teens and young adults often face moments of doubt, unsure of what they stand for or where their boundaries lie within social circles. It's a confusing period when you're trying to fit in while figuring out your own identity. Imagine being at a party with friends and feeling the pressure to laugh at a joke that doesn't resonate with you or engage in activities that make you uncomfortable. It's easy to go along with the crowd, but deep down, a part of you yearns for authenticity and self-acceptance.

This chapter will dive into the essential practice of knowing yourself first as the cornerstone of a healthy social life. We will explore how understanding your core values, emotions, and personal boundaries can help you build genuine confidence and positively navigate social interactions. By integrating mindfulness into these practices, you'll find a balanced approach to maintaining authenticity while connecting meaningfully with others.

Self-mastery

Understanding yourself is like building a foundation for a house. You wouldn't want to live in a house that felt shaky or unstable, right? That same principle applies to your social life. By identifying your core values, emotions, and personal boundaries, you create a solid base for all your future interactions. For teens and young adults, this is incredibly important because it sets the tone for authentic connections with others. Imagine knowing exactly what you stand for and feeling confident enough to express it. Doesn't that feel empowering?

Start by digging into your core values. These are the principles you hold most dearly. They drive your decisions and shape how you interact with the world. For instance, if you value honesty, you'll likely gravitate towards people who are straightforward and transparent. Conversely, being around someone who lies might trigger discomfort. To explore your own values, try a journaling exercise where you list moments that made you proud of yourself. What standards were you holding in those moments? Which ones inspired you to act that way? Identifying your values helps align your friendships and relationships with what's truly important to you.

Next, let's consider emotions. Emotions can be tricky, especially when you're not used to working with them. Yet, they communicate critical information about our needs and boundaries. Think about a time you felt unexpectedly angry. Was there a boundary crossed? Figuring out your emotional triggers is a fantastic way to understand what makes you tick. Write down situations or phrases that spark strong emotional reactions. For instance, if being ignored makes you angry, explore why that bothers you. This could reveal a need to be seen and heard, central to a value of connectedness.

Setting personal boundaries is the third pillar of self-awareness. Boundaries define where you end and someone else begins. They protect your mental and emotional well-being by outlining acceptable and unacceptable behaviors. Consider a friend who texts late at night, disrupting your sleep. A boundary here might be limiting phone interactions after a certain time. Practicing saying "no" when something doesn't feel right aligns your interactions with personal comfort levels. By establishing these limits, you respect yourself and, in turn, foster relationships that respect you.

Journaling can be a powerful tool here as well. Start by listing times you felt uncomfortable or violated. What was happening? Who was involved? More importantly, what boundary did this reveal? Move on to articulate that boundary by writing, "I need...," for example, "I need my space respected during study time." Consistently revisiting your boundaries ensures they remain relevant as you grow.

Integrating these practices offers more than just self-awareness. It ushers in a pathway toward mindfulness. When you know your inner world, mindfulness becomes a smoother journey. You become acutely aware of the present, harnessing insights rooted in your values, emotions, and boundaries. For instance, understanding that lack of communication triggers anxiety helps you develop mindfulness strategies to cope with tension in social settings. You might employ deep breathing exercises to maintain calm or practice active listening, knowing it fulfills your need for rapport.

Consider reflection exercises that build this foundation. Asking yourself daily questions can deepen your understanding: "What am I feeling right now?" or "Did my actions today align with my values?" Over time, these queries turn into a habit, bringing clarity and a sense of control over how you interact with others. Eventually, this awareness seeps into all facets of life, from relationships to career choices, creating an authentic presence grounded in self-knowledge.

Let's get practical with an exercise about emotional triggers. Step one: identify an emotional reaction you experience at least once a week. It could be anger when someone interrupts you. Write this down. Step two: connect this reaction to personal values. What does the interruption say about what you value? If it's respect and consideration, you now understand that conversations with mutual respect are crucial for your comfort. This simple task lays the groundwork for understanding what drives your emotions.

There's something beautifully liberating about knowing your needs and values. It equips you with the ability to advocate for yourself. When someone crosses your boundaries, a firm yet friendly, "I prefer if you didn't do that," sends a message loud and clear. Plus, having this self-awareness encourages empathy. You become more attuned to others' boundaries and emotions, creating a loop of understanding that enriches all interactions.

Self-awareness sharpens your inner compass. It holds you steady amidst societal pressures, guiding you to make choices that honor your true self. Once you embrace your values, emotions, and boundaries, you engage in social interactions with authenticity. This authenticity is attractive to others, creating deeper and more meaningful connections. It's like sending out a beacon to the world that says, "This is who I am, and I'm confident in it."

As you explore these self-awareness practices, remember they are not meant to confine you. Instead, they form the backbone of a life lived with intention and presence. Every realization is a steppingstone towards more profound mindfulness, which we'll dive deeper into next. Your journey begins here, and the path promises to be as rewarding as it is enlightening. Enjoy the exploration.

Moments and Environments

Recognizing moments when we compromise our authenticity often begins with a simple realization: the little changes we make in ourselves to fit in can slowly shape how we feel and who we become. This awareness is pivotal because it informs the kinds of connections we build. Picture this: You're hanging out with friends, and someone tells a joke you don't find funny, but you laugh along because everyone else does. These small moments might feel insignificant, but over time, they add up and can erode your sense of self.

This is where mindfulness comes in handy. It allows you to pause in these situations and decide whether your reaction aligns with your true feelings or values. Imagine standing at the crossroads of reacting automatically or responding thoughtfully. By practicing mindfulness, you learn to take a breath before reacting, giving you the space to choose your path with intention, so you can remain true to who you are.

When it comes to relationships, knowing and honoring your values sets the tone for genuine interactions. Recognizing what's important to you is like planting a flag for your identity. It signals to others where you stand, helping attract those who respect and share similar values. Conversely, compromising your authenticity in these interactions can lead to shallow relationships based on a false version of yourself, which is inherently fragile.

The practice of mindfulness fosters genuine confidence. It enables you to express yourself without fear of judgment because you are certain about your personal values and boundaries. You can engage with others fully present, valuing their perspectives while staying true to your own. This approach not only strengthens your self-esteem but also your connections, as people appreciate authenticity and often are inspired by it.

To begin this journey, start by recognizing when you feel the urge to conform to others' expectations. Check in with yourself during social interactions. Ask if you're being true to your beliefs or just going with the flow. An example could be declining to participate in a conversation topic that makes you uncomfortable, even if everyone else is deeply engaged. Imagine a scenario where peers are discussing something contentious, and you feel pressured to agree just to keep peace. Mindfulness encourages you to voice your perspective respectfully, which nurtures trust and mutual respect within your social group.

The essence of maintaining authenticity during peer interactions is not just about resistance; it's about reforming how you interact with those pressures. Let's look at a common scene: a friend asks you to do something you're not comfortable with, like skipping class. Without thinking, you might feel inclined to say yes. Mindfulness invites you to pause and consider your response. Is this something you want, or is it an imposition on your boundaries?

Taking this further, one effective mindfulness exercise is to practice 'Thoughtful Deliberation.' In social settings, before responding, mentally ask yourself three questions: Does this choice reflect my true self? Will it respect my values? Am I feeling pressured? For instance, if you face peer pressure to wear something you're uncomfortable with, apply this exercise to decide if you're doing it for acceptance or because it genuinely pleases you.

Another method is to practice 'Reflective Journaling' after significant interactions. Write down instances where you felt you compromised your authenticity and analyze why this happened. Consider alternative responses that align better with your values. This practice enhances your awareness, making you more prepared to respond authentically in the future.

Mindfulness is not just about awareness but building resilience too. By consistently recognizing and managing situations that test your authenticity, you build an internal strength that makes it easier to stay genuine in any social dynamic. Think of it like working out; the more you practice, the stronger you become. Over time, these mindful responses become second nature, allowing you to navigate peer pressure with grace and confidence.

And spotting emotional discomfort just might be your cue that authenticity is slipping. When you feel uneasy, it's often your subconscious nudging you back to your core values. Pay attention to these signals. They can guide you to course correct before losing sight of who you are. It's about using these feelings to bolster your relationships, creating connections grounded in honesty.

By examining real-life examples, such as when you resist the trend of social media personas that don't resonate with you, mindfulness becomes your tool for liberation. Choose not to follow every viral trend or broadcast a curated online self just to gain likes. Instead, use mindfulness to cultivate self-acceptance, allowing you to express an online presence that's as genuine as your offline one. This kind of resilience not only protects your authenticity but also makes you a role model for others facing similar pressures.

As you embrace mindfulness as a daily practice, it sets the stage perfectly for evolving conversations and staying present in the face of peer pressure. It prepares you to engage fully, allowing you to be an active participant rather than a passive reactor. This foundation of self-awareness and authenticity then becomes the steppingstone for enhancing your social interactions, ensuring that they are not just polite exchanges, but meaningful connections rooted in truth and mutual respect.

Mindfulness Revisited

Mindfulness acts as a radar that helps detect social red flags or emotional discomfort in conversations, especially when facing peer pressure. It allows us to anchor ourselves in the present, helping us maintain authenticity and providing room for thoughtful responses instead of knee-jerk reactions. Fortunately, several tools can help nurture this form of awareness. Let's look at these methods and break down how they work in everyday life situations, thus fortifying your understanding of self and social dynamics.

Body Scan Technique

The body scan focuses on bringing your attention to bodily sensations, which often mirror your emotional state and can subtly signal discomfort during peer pressure.

Find a quiet place: Situate yourself in a comfortable position, closing your eyes if that feels right.

Take a deep breath: Allow yourself to relax, feeling your body sink into the chair.

Start at the top of your head: Mentally scan downwards, observing any sensations (tightness, warmth, tingling) without judgment.

Move slowly through your whole body: Visit areas like the shoulders, chest, arms, all the way to your toes. Acknowledge the feelings instead of seeking to change them.

Use your breath to release tension: Upon identifying areas of tension, imagine warmth and relaxation enveloping them as you exhale.

Contextual example: During a party, a friend urges you to participate in an activity you're unsure about. Excuse yourself for a moment, head to a restroom or quiet corner and perform a brief body scan. If significant tension rests in your chest, it could be your intuition indicating unease with the activity, helping guide your next decision.

Mindful Breathing

Mindful breathing directly connects you with the present moment, maintaining your focus and calming anxiety that may arise in pressuring situations.

Deep inhale: Breathe in slowly through your nose, counting to four.

Pause briefly: Hold your breath for a count of two.

Controlled exhale: Release slowly through your mouth, counting to six.

Repeat the cycle three more times: Let your focus stay on the rise and fall of your chest, absorbing any peacefulness that comes with each breath.

Contextual example: Engrossed in a lunch table debate that's turning heated, you practice mindful breathing. Your inner calm contrasts the chaotic energy, supporting you to voice your opinion clearly when prompted. The practice strengthens your self-trust, ensuring peer dynamics don't override your feelings.

Observational Awareness

Observational awareness involves consciously paying attention to the interactions and subtle signals around you, setting the stage for more genuine and understanding responses.

Start by observing participants' body language: Notice cues such as crossed arms or lack of eye contact hinting discomfort or disengagement.

Listen actively: Focus on not only what is said but how it's expressed, including tone and inflections.

Tune into group dynamics: Spots where you feel an ebb or wave from the group, be it emotional or energetic, can signal collective pressure or hesitation.

Acknowledge internal reactions: Identify how these observations affect your comfort level and decision-making process.

Contextual example: During a group discussion, accusations fly, someone lowering their head suggests they feel attacked. By honing your observational skills, you coax further dialogue to ease tension. Seeing peers mirror your approach promotes a more thoughtful, inclusive atmosphere.

Self-Inquiry and Reflection

This complements mindfulness by probing into why certain situations spark specific emotions or thoughts, offering clarity on personal boundaries and values.

Identify situations that frequently cause discomfort: Which environments or peer suggestions bring hesitation or distress?

Question internal dialogue: What are your thoughts when confronted with differing opinions or pressures? Are they protective or limiting?

Regular journaling practice: Integrate journal time to explore past interactions, discerning patterns about behaviors you're proud of and those needing adjustment.

Contextual example: After a night out with new acquaintances, you journal about feeling hesitant when discussions shifted to weekend plans you deemed irresponsible. Exploring your motives for hesitation, like wanting to preserve personal safety and limits, reinforces self-assurance against similar future pressures.

Grounding Techniques

Grounding exercises distract from overwhelming sensations, focusing on the present to deter anxiety or discomfort from making decisions for you.

Engage the five senses: Name five things you see, hear, touch, taste, and smell. This immersive involvement grounds you.

Mentally affirm inner footing: Repeat a calming statement, like "I am present and aware," reminding yourself that you're anchored.

Create a sensory toolkit: Keep a small item with texture in your pocket, touching it during tense exchanges to direct focus away from stress.

Contextual example: While experiencing an unexpected confrontation about a rumor at school, you engage the senses by describing wall colors, the noise level, and the crunch of your apple. Focusing outward composes your nerves, addressing the confrontation with steadiness and poise.

Integrating these tools into your day-to-day conversations and encounters shields you from the sway of peer pressure by ensuring your responses remain aligned with your authentic self. Each practice carries you closer to understanding your emotions and needs while maintaining peace in social engagements. Recognizing when mindfulness propels your self-awareness strengthens confidence, foreshadowing the seamless transition into future explorations of genuine confidence and humility.

Emotional Collection

It's crucial to build on our earlier conversation regarding the power of staying present during social interactions. You may recall that this involves recognizing social red flags and emotional discomfort in real time. When you notice these signals, you switch from reacting impulsively to responding in a measured, thoughtful way. It's like tapping into an internal pause button that offers you a moment to assess and choose how to proceed. By harnessing self-awareness, you unlock the door to genuine confidence. This approach means understanding your emotions and triggers, allowing you to engage with others from a place of calm and clarity.

Think of self-awareness as a bridge to quiet strength. If we picture confidence, it's easy to envision someone loud and assertive. Yet true confidence often speaks softly. It's the calm assurance that doesn't need to shout for attention. Quiet strength emphasizes listening and comprehending rather than dominating conversations. This kind of confidence respects others' perspectives while still valuing one's own voice. It's invaluable in shaping meaningful relationships since others sense when interactions are genuine and mutual, not self-centered, or overly assertive.

To illustrate, imagine you're in a group discussion, and someone makes a point you disagree with. A loud arrogance might lead you to interrupt and overwhelm the dialogue. On the other hand, quiet strength would involve listening fully before offering your perspective. You acknowledge their view, then clearly present your own. In doing so, you maintain a respectful space for dialogue. This behavior models confidence that welcomes understanding over mere winning of an argument.

This approach also prioritizes self-respect. When you respect yourself, you're less inclined to seek approval through people-pleasing. Operating from a place of respect allows you to set boundaries, addressing the tendency many have to bend at any discomfort or pressure. When you hold self-respect, you resist the pull of codependency, where your sense of worth relies on others' opinions. Standing firm in your values and needs doesn't mean you disregard others; it means you navigate social dynamics with integrity to both yourself and those you interact with.

Practical strategies for expressing confidence include using "I" statements to communicate feelings or needs without assigning blame. For instance, saying "I feel overlooked when my contributions aren't acknowledged" instead of "You never listen to me" shifts the focus to your personal experience. This method fosters understanding, allowing others to see your perspective without feeling attacked.

Imagine a scenario at school where a group project becomes unbalanced. One member isn't contributing, causing friction. Instead of confronting aggressively, you might approach the individual privately and express your concern: "I've noticed you haven't had the chance to contribute as much. Is there anything I can do to support you?" This strategy opens a dialogue and shows initiative without aggression. You make the first move toward collaborative problem-solving, which builds trust and respect in your group.

Building authentic relationships also involves learning when to speak and when to listen. Practice active listening by maintaining eye contact, nodding in agreement, or offering verbal affirmations like "I see" or "That's interesting." These cues signal your engagement and make people feel valued in conversations. Over time, these small practices enhance your empathy and help you read social cues more accurately.

As you practice these skills, remember it's normal to feel unsure at times. No one embodies genuine confidence all the time, and that's human. Instead of retreating, reflect on what you can learn from each interaction. Perhaps you spoke too quickly in a tense moment or hesitated when you wanted to voice an idea. Use these moments as insights. They help tweak and improve how you present yourself in social settings.

Moreover, the quiet strength approach reinforces your mental energy for what truly matters. You conserve emotional resources by not engaging in unnecessary conflicts or trying to control others' opinions. You find freedom in valuing your authenticity over external validation. This mindset naturally attracts others who appreciate and respect you for who you are, fostering stronger, more real connections.

As you find your true voice, let it guide your social interactions. Trust that self-awareness gives you the tools to weather social storms with grace and conviction. It's a lifelong journey where setbacks introduce opportunities for growth, not failures. Practicing this balance leads to enriched, healthier relationships and an inner confidence that needs no external endorsement.

Lessons Learned

As we conclude this exploration into self-awareness and mindfulness, it's evident that knowing yourself deeply and practicing mindfulness are the cornerstones of building genuine confidence. By understanding your core values, emotions, and boundaries, you create authentic connections with others that withstand peer pressure and social challenges. Mindfulness offers a crucial pause, allowing you to respond thoughtfully rather than react impulsively in diverse situations. As you practice these techniques, remember that true confidence often embodies quiet strength, leading to more meaningful conversations and relationships. Now that you've begun this journey, embrace the lifelong process of growing self-awareness. In doing so, you'll continue to foster enriching interactions grounded in authenticity, setting the stage for a future where you navigate life with clarity and poise.

BOUNDARIES, CONSENT, AND THE ART OF "YES" AND "NO"

Have you ever felt uneasy in a crowded room, unable to pinpoint why someone's presence made your skin crawl? Or maybe you've hesitated to share a part of yourself with a friend, fearing their reaction might be less than supportive. These moments, though small, are signals that our boundaries, those invisible lines that keep us safe and respected, are crucial but often neglected. Recognizing the importance of these cues isn't always straightforward, especially when social pressures blur our instincts. Why do we struggle to assert our needs, and how do we navigate saying 'yes' or 'no' when every fiber of our being demands clarity?

Whether it's your best friend overstepping personal spaces at a party or feeling overwhelmed by digital demands that invade your peace, understanding your limits isn't just about self-preservation; it's about fostering healthier, more respectful interactions. In this chapter, we aim to unravel the complexities of setting boundaries, mastering consent, and developing the art of agreeing and refusing graciously. By exploring these dynamics, we'll discover ways to reinforce our sense of self-worth and ensure our relationships are grounded in mutual respect and understanding.

What Are Boundaries (And Why Do They Matter)?

Boundaries help you define what is acceptable for you in all aspects of life. Understanding and establishing them allows you to preserve your personal well-being and ensures respectful interactions with others. Emotional boundaries, for instance, refer to recognizing and respecting your own and others' feelings. You encounter them when someone expects you to share personal details or emotional intimacy that you're not comfortable disclosing. Imagine your friend pressuring you to talk about a painful experience you're not ready to discuss. Recognizing when you feel uncomfortable or overwhelmed helps you establish a clear emotional boundary. Being firm about not participating in a conversation that crosses these lines helps you protect your mental and emotional health.

Physical boundaries pertain to your personal space and physical contact. You likely encounter situations where these need to be respected. Picture being at a crowded party where someone continues to touch your shoulder despite your discomfort. Acknowledging this feeling and asserting your need for space is crucial for your well-being. It's okay to politely ask someone to give you more personal space or to stop touching you if it makes you uncomfortable. Knowing when physical boundaries are crossed draws the line between feeling safe and vulnerable.

In today's digital world, digital boundaries have become increasingly important. They involve how you engage with technology, social media, and online communication. Reflect on moments when friends post images or stories of you on social media without your permission. This may not always reflect your online identity or comfort level. In such cases, communicating openly about your preferences can maintain your well-being. Setting digital boundaries could involve asking friends not to tag you in photos or discussing what content you're comfortable sharing with colleagues online.

Energetic boundaries relate to how you manage your energy in social situations. Imagine feeling drained after spending time with certain people or in specific environments. These boundaries help you identify when interactions leave you emotionally depleted. A close friend constantly seeking advice on every trivial problem might leave you feeling exhausted. Setting limits on these interactions protects your energy and ensures you replenish it when needed.

Being aware of boundary violations is critical. Recognizing discomfort, resentment, or anxiety when engaging with others often signals a boundary issue. When your friend repeatedly interrupts you during conversations, you may feel anger bubbling up. Addressing this ensures you respect your communication space. Expressing these feelings to your friends helps recalibrate mutual respect in your interactions. Likewise, when someone dismisses your refusal by saying, "Come on, don't be silly," after you declined an invitation, they're not considering your boundaries. Reasserting your stance fortifies your limits and communicates that they should be honored.

Young adults and teens are often under pressure from peers or authority figures to overlook boundaries. For instance, at school, you might feel compelled to lend a classmate your notebook even when it's inconvenient. Recognizing that loaning your materials affects your available resources serves as an essential aspect of maintaining boundaries. Similarly, peer pressure at parties may push you to drink more than you're comfortable with. Trusting your initial instinct to refuse helps you stay true to your boundaries. Articulating that choice with confidence reinforces self-respect and personal limits.

You learn about boundaries and their significance as you experience different situations. Conversations about respecting personal limits lay the groundwork for trust. They empower you to be assertive when necessary. You foster a culture of respect where mutual understanding is key. Take the time to observe your emotions and analyze various interaction dynamics. Listening to your instincts is the first step toward establishing clear boundaries.

Maintaining transparency about your boundaries in relationships builds an atmosphere of respect and trust. It strengthens connections and helps prevent resentment from crashing in later. Having open dialogues about emotional needs, physical space, digital presence, and energy preservation fosters healthy exchanges. Practicing active listening, empathy, and support for others further enriches these interactions. People appreciate clarity, so you can discuss your boundaries with friends, partners, and family members. Engaging in ongoing conversations around boundaries improves mutual understanding.

Imagine being in a relationship where partners openly share what they are comfortable with. Without judgement, they accept each other's perspectives and limits. Both parties respect differences and embrace the boundaries set in place. This mutual understanding creates a harmonious environment based on trust and consent.

Consider situations where people dismiss your boundaries as trivial. This highlights the need to be assertive in reinforcing them. Responding with clarity and honesty when faced with challenging situations ensures your boundaries remain intact. However, there are moments you encounter individuals who fail to respect these lines. Knowing how to express yourself and saying "no" confidently becomes essential. This proficiency in asserting boundaries, be it with friends, at work, or during social gatherings, underlines your autonomy and promotes self-esteem.

Transitioning to the upcoming section focuses on understanding and dealing with those who ignore boundaries. You'll also explore practical scripts for firmly saying "no" in various contexts, be it at a party, when asked for favors, in dating scenarios, or during online exchanges. These tools equip you to handle boundary violations effectively. Familiarizing yourself with these scripts enhances your ability to protect yourself and assert your needs. Feeling empowered to defend your boundaries lays the groundwork for building healthier and more respectful relationships. Developing the skill of saying "no" when needed serves as the keystone for an authentic life aligned with your values and comfort.

Saying "No" Without Guilt (and "Yes" Without Fear)

Boundaries hold immense power in shaping the quality of our relationships and interactions. They're not just lines on a map, but active measures of respect we extend towards ourselves and demand from others. Imagine your boundaries as an invisible shield, dynamic and strong, designed to protect your well-being. At the core of this concept is a simple truth: people who don't respect your boundaries shouldn't have access to you.

This idea connects directly to the foundational steps of self-awareness and self-assertion, crucial to recognizing when your comfort zones are breached. This awareness forms the bedrock of protecting your personal space, allowing you to articulate and maintain these boundaries with confidence. When people push past your limits or dismiss them, it's not just an inconvenience; it's an infringement on your self-worth.

Disrespecting boundaries signals a lack of respect for you as an individual. When someone disregards your expressed needs, it demonstrates that they see their own desires as more important than your comfort and safety. This is why boundary violators shouldn't be given a free pass into your life. Their continual presence can erode your sense of self-respect and compromise the healthiness of your relationships.

Learning to say "no" is a cornerstone of protecting what matters to you. It can feel intimidating to turn someone down, especially if you're worried about how they might react. Yet, standing firm on your boundaries is a form of self-respect and a statement of your values. Let's explore practical ways to articulate a thoughtful yet decisive "no," empowering you to maintain the autonomy you deserve.

Start by considering this method: when you need to say "no," begin with empathy, clearly state your decision, and close with gratitude or an offer of alternative help if appropriate. For instance, in a party setting, you could commit to practicing this script: "Thank you for thinking of me, but I won't be able to attend the party. I hope it's a great success." This conveys your message respectfully and assertively.

If someone pressures you into sharing personal information online, try reiterating your boundaries: "I prefer not to share details about that. I appreciate your understanding." This straightforward approach not only communicates your stance but also implies mutual respect, key components of any relationship worth nurturing.

Dating can be particularly challenging when expressing boundaries. Feel empowered to say, "I'm flattered you're interested, but I'm not looking to date right now." Saying this clearly avoids any ambiguity and reinforces your autonomy over your own availability and openness to romantic involvement.

When friends or peers ask for favors that overextend you, it's vital to express your limitations without feeling guilty. For requests that strain your time or resources, consider this response: "I won't be able to help with that this time. I have other commitments." This provides a clear boundary without inviting negotiation, saving you from resentment or burnout.

To practice these skills, try implementing a simple five-step exercise. First, identify the situation where you feel your boundaries are easily crossed. Recognize the physical and emotional sensations that arise, do your shoulders tense up, do you feel anxious? Next, formulate phrases that fit your voice and comfort level. Practice saying them in front of a mirror or with friends who respect your boundaries. Then, anticipate possible responses and rehearse maintaining your boundary regardless. Finally, trust in the power of your "no" and observe how interactions change over time. This method not only strengthens your ability to assert boundaries but also reinforces your understanding of why maintaining them is crucial.

Setting boundaries isn't just about saying "no"; it's about cultivating an environment where your needs are respected and upheld as a standard. Asserting these boundaries may initially challenge some relationships, but long term, they foster connections built on mutual respect and understanding.

Remember, every time you uphold your boundaries with resolution and without apology, you reinforce your self-worth. The strongest relationships, be they friendships, family ties, or romantic bonds, thrive on this foundation of reciprocal respect. With these strategies, you're equipped to navigate your world with clarity and assurance, establishing that your boundaries are as inviolable as your own sense of self-respect.

Navigating Consent and Mutual Respect

Setting personal boundaries serves as a crucial skill for teens and young adults, with each boundary acting like a protective shield around their life. When individuals disregard these boundaries, it underscores their lack of respect for one's autonomy, clearly marking why such individuals do not merit a space in your life. By holding boundaries, you teach others how to treat you, reinforcing that your time and energy are valuable resources. This lesson empowers young people to generate an internal blueprint for confidence that resonates in various social situations.

Navigating the art of saying "no" without guilt is a pivotal step in affirming self-respect. It involves understanding that "no" is a complete sentence. When attending social events, it's easy to feel pressured into saying yes. However, reflecting on personal values helps determine when a no is appropriate. Consider a party invitation at a time when you need to study or rest. Courteously declining by saying, "I need some downtime," is a powerful act of self-care.

Conversely, saying "yes" to opportunities that align with your goals can be an adventure. For instance, saying yes to a group project that challenges your skills or interests may open new doors. Assess situations based on your current capacity and interests, ensuring your decisions support your growth. Whether it's taking up a leadership role in a club or volunteering for a cause you care about, these choices can bring fulfillment. Both "no" and "yes" can contribute positively to your life when they are congruent with your desires.

Peer pressure can often cloud judgment, especially in dating scenarios and gatherings. It's vital to practice self-assertion with conviction. Let's take dating as an example. If a partner suggests something that doesn't feel right to you, articulate your boundary clearly. Say, "I'm not ready for this, and I need to be comfortable with my choices." This articulation not only reinforces your stance, but it also sets a precedent for future interactions.

Clear, simple language aids in creating firm boundaries, while consistency ensures these boundaries are respected. Role-playing scenarios can aid in bolstering confidence. Practicing phrases like, "I'm focusing on my goals right now," or "This isn't for me," prepares you for varied situations. You're allowed to redefine the boundaries as you grow and determine which people or situations are worthy of your energy.

The benefits of upholding personal boundaries manifest in the form of empowerment and self-assurance. Allowing yourself to prioritize your own comfort and needs creates a ripple effect of positivity. Peers start seeing you as someone who respects themselves, thus inspiring them to do the same. This practice also encourages healthier friendships. Peers who genuinely value you will respect your decisions. Such friendships flourish under the mutual understanding that each person's wellbeing is paramount.

For those who struggle with offending others by setting boundaries, remember that true friends will respect your "no" just as much as they'll appreciate your "yes." It's about establishing a rapport grounded in mutual respect, where both parties understand the value of genuine regard. In social dynamics, it's common to face backlash from those unused to hearing no. Stay firm and be consistent with your boundaries, understanding that discomfort often signifies necessary personal growth.

Moving from a micro to a macro perspective, recognizing boundary violations in group settings becomes essential. In club meetings or group outings, contributing to discussions about respect and consent can strengthen group ethics. Assertively upholding your boundaries openly encourages others to respect theirs, leading to a culture of mutual regard.

At the same time, identifying opportunities worth pursuing demands discernment. Differentiating between obligations and genuine interests enhances life experiences. For instance, differentiate between obligatory engagements and those that genuinely excite you. Choosing activities that align with your aspirations leads to satisfaction and personal development. By consciously selecting paths that resonate with your inner goals, you create a path that aligns with your purpose.

As we transition to the upcoming discussion on consent, understanding its foundations rests heavily on respecting boundaries. Asking for and giving consent requires clarity, kindness, and firmness. Articulate your consent similarly to how you express your boundaries: directly and without apologizing. Let's say a friend invites you to join a spontaneous adventure. "Thanks for inviting me. I'll pass this time, but let's hang out another day," preserves your autonomy while keeping the door open for future connections.

In situations where someone challenges your boundaries, identify your comfort level first. Kindly but firmly assert your stance. This approach not only preserves relationships but also reinforces your commitment to self-respect. Friendships, romance, and peer interactions thrive under an unspoken agreement of mutual respect. By continuously practicing these principles, you embark on a journey toward fulfilling and respectful connections.

Fostering an environment where boundaries and consent coexist underpins healthy interactions. By implementing these practices consistently, you showcase and promote a culture of respect. These interactions represent an ongoing dialogue that empowers you and your peers to grow in a thriving community. The understanding and respect of boundaries ultimately pave the way for more meaningful conversations about consent, enriching life's tapestry with threads of respect and self-worth.

Digital Boundaries and Social Media Etiquette

In the previous section, we explored overcoming guilt associated with saying "no" and recognizing when to say "yes" in alignment with personal values. These insights prepare us to delve into the intricate dynamics of consent in our relationships. At its core, consent is about respecting boundaries through dialogue. Consent is fundamental to friendships, romances, and everyday interactions, shaping healthier dynamics while preventing potential tensions.

Imagine friendships where mutual understanding and respect are cultivated. This happens when we clarify our needs and listen to others. For example, in a friendship, discussing comfort levels about sharing personal information can strengthen the bond. It shows both parties care about each other's peace of mind. In romantic relationships, consent transcends being a one-time question. It's a consistent, ongoing conversation. Let's say two individuals are exploring a new aspect of their relationship. Asking questions like "Is this okay with you?" or "How are you feeling about this?" becomes vital. These questions show consideration and attentiveness. They also set a tone for honesty and openness.

Let's move into strategies for asking for and giving consent. Being clear, kind, and firm helps avoid misunderstandings. When asking for consent, using straightforward language is crucial. Rather than assuming someone is comfortable with a situation, simply ask. "Would you like to do this?" or "Is this something you're okay with?" Such phrases prevent assumptions and create room for honest responses.

Equally important is how we respond when someone seeks our consent. Listening actively and expressing true feelings can be empowering. Saying "I don't feel comfortable with that" or "I'd prefer if we didn't" establishes boundaries while being respectful. It reassures everyone involved that honesty rules the interaction.

But what if someone doesn't respect these boundaries? Asserting oneself becomes necessary. Declining persistently "I said no, and I mean it," is crucial. It's also vital to reach out to trusted friends, mentors, or professionals for support. They can offer guidance and reassurance in maintaining boundaries. More so, practicing assertiveness in less critical scenarios, like declining a party invitation, strengthens confidence and prepares us for more challenging situations.

Digital boundaries are as crucial as personal ones. Maintaining online serenity requires strategic actions like unfollowing or muting accounts causing distress. It's not about being hostile; it's about protecting one's peace. Blocking should be a last resort, used when other measures fall short. Each action conveys a silent yet powerful message: personal space is sacred.

Screen-time limits further support emotional balance. They act as boundaries, protecting us from digital overload. Establishing specific times to disconnect from devices fosters mental clarity and reduces stress. For instance, setting a digital curfew an hour before bedtime aids better sleep. It minimizes exposure to stimulating content and promotes relaxation. Weekends or vacations offer opportunities for digital detoxes, allowing time for hobbies, family, and reflection.

Oversharing is a gateway to vulnerability. It risks privacy and emotional well-being. Let's say you share a detailed account of a personal challenge online. It might offer temporary relief but invites unsolicited opinions. Limiting the depth and detail of what we share online protects our privacy. Engaging sincerely in face-to-face conversations provides support without involving a faceless audience.

Reclaiming digital privacy begins with examining our online presence. How much of our personal information is available, and to whom? Reviewing privacy settings on social media platforms ensures sensitive details are concealed from unwanted viewers. Mutual respect in these digital interactions, much like in real life, reinforces the foundation of trust and safety.

Digital safety ties back to consent in our relationships. When sharing photos or events involving others, ask for permission first. A simple "Do you mind if I post this?" shows respect for their boundaries. It fosters an environment where consent is naturally part of every interaction, whether digital or personal.

Not respecting these digital norms can lead to misunderstandings or conflicts. Open dialogue helps address these issues. Engaging the other party by expressing how their actions affect you can de-escalate tensions. When a friend overshares a private conversation online, addressing it directly shows maturity. "I felt uncomfortable with that post. Can we discuss this?" is one way to resolve the concern while reinforcing boundaries.

This segues into another point: the significance of explaining our boundaries. It's not just about stating them but providing context, when appropriate, so others understand why they matter. Saying, "I need this time for myself to recharge" explains the boundary without being defensive, fostering an empathetic response.

The journey through understanding and applying consent is ongoing. It's a conscious choice to respect both ourselves and the people around us. Concrete strategies like asking clear, respectful questions; setting personal and digital boundaries; limiting screen time; and protecting our private information are practical tools in this pursuit. Each choice we make fosters a culture grounded in mutual respect and open communication.

As we integrate these strategies into our daily lives, we discover the profound impact on our relationships. They become richer, more authentic, and healthier. It's about striving for balance, knowing when to say "yes" joyfully and when to voice a firm, kind "no." These small yet significant steps reaffirm our commitment to personal and collective well-being, ensuring our interactions leave us feeling respected and valued.

Concluding Thoughts

In understanding the significance of boundaries, teens and young adults can transform their interactions into healthier ones marked by respect and consent. With boundaries serving as protective shields, they help us manage our personal space and well-being across emotional, physical, digital, and energetic dimensions. Now that we realize their importance, we can confidently say "no" when pressured yet embrace valuable opportunities that truly resonate with us. This balance builds self-esteem, teaching others how to treat us with the respect we deserve. As we venture further, exploring practical ways of asserting our boundaries and the art of saying "no," we empower ourselves to cultivate more authentic connections. By reinforcing these principles in daily life, we not only enrich our personal experiences but also foster a respectful and considerate culture around us.

CHAPTER 16

FINDING YOUR CIRCLE, HOW TO BUILD TRUST AND FRIENDSHIPS THAT LAST

Raul sat alone in the crowded cafeteria, fiddling with his phone. Around him, laughter and animated conversations filled the air as clusters of students shared stories from their weekend adventures. Despite being surrounded by familiar faces, Raul felt a gnawing loneliness. He had acquaintances in abundance but struggled to call any one of them a true friend. The connections he craved seemed elusive, slipping through the cracks of casual talks and fleeting moments. It wasn't for lack of trying either; he'd been to parties, joined clubs, even attended study groups, all in hopes of building something real and lasting. Yet, time after time, he found himself back at square one, wondering what he was missing.

This experience isn't unique to Raul. Many people find themselves in similar situations, surrounded yet somehow separate, wanting deeper connections but not knowing how to cultivate them. Everyone wants friends they can trust, who make them feel safe, and bring joy into their lives, but building such meaningful relationships involves more than just proximity or shared interests. In this chapter, we will delve into the essential elements of creating friendships that stand the test of time, exploring what makes these bonds strong and enduring.

What Real Friendship Looks Like

Friendships can be a source of immense joy and comfort, but building lasting ones requires real effort and understanding. The backbone of any meaningful friendship relies on safety, honesty, laughter, and support.

Safety is the foundation where friends create an environment that is free from judgment and harm. When you feel a sense of safety with someone, you know you can express yourself without fear of ridicule. This mutual trust nurtures a relationship. Consider a friend who listens without judgment and offers thoughtful feedback when you're in a situation that requires a difficult decision. They respect your boundaries and offer a shoulder without expecting anything in return. This nurturing environment of safety becomes a fertile ground for a long-lasting friendship, where both people can grow and help each other in life.

Honesty comes next. Real friendships thrive on truthfulness. When someone is truthful, they don't sugarcoat the truth or paint a misleading picture. Imagine a friend who tells you when you've made a mistake but does so with the intention of helping you become a better person. Their honesty signifies their investment in the friendship. This open line of communication stems from an understanding that honesty is about authenticity, grounding the relationship in something real rather than superficial pretenses. This authenticity is magnetic, drawing people deeper into the relationship.

Laughter adds the spark that keeps a friendship lively. When you share laughter, you share joy, lightening burdens, and deepening connections. Laughter can bridge the gap between rough patches. Ever noticed how an inside joke can lighten the tension in a challenging moment? It acts like a bomb, reminding you of shared experiences and the joy that living life together can bring. Laughter, even in the face of adversity, keeps friendships buoyant and fun.

Support lies as a constant backdrop in good friendships. It is the steadfast element that involves being there when times are tough. True friends support each other through life's ups and downs, whether it be in the form of a pep talk before an exam or staying up late to talk through a crisis. They celebrate your victories and commiserate over losses. This mutual support forms an unwavering commitment to each other's well-being, forming a fabric of togetherness.

However, to truly cultivate these genuine connections, understanding friendship green flags versus red flags helps. Seeing green flags means spotting positive signs, like consistent communication, mutual respect, and empathy. For instance, if a friend remembers small details about a conversation you had, it shows their genuine interest and care. They apologize when they're wrong, showing humility and a willingness to repair any disagreements.

Red flags, on the other hand, indicate potential problems. Beware if someone constantly drains your energy or makes you feel lesser than you are. These are signs of a toxic, potentially harmful friendship. If a friend only reaches out when they need something but disappears when roles are reversed, that's a red flag. Recognizing these flags empowers you to refocus your energies on relationships that enrich your life, not complicate it.

Now, it's crucial to understand that the chase for popularity can often cloud judgment. When a focus is placed solely on the number of connections you have rather than their quality, you risk spreading yourself too thin to truly enjoy any meaningful ones. Building true friendships isn't about amassing numbers but about fostering relationships that matter.

Pursuing popularity can lead you to overlook valuable friendships. Society often encourages valuing popularity, but have you ever pondered the richness found in deep, meaningful connections over mere numbers? Studies show that people with a few close friendships experience higher satisfaction and emotional well-being, compared to those with a wide but shallow network. It is those genuine connections that last a lifetime, a core group that laughs, supports, is honest, and makes you feel safe.

The focus should then be on authentic relationships, ones based on mutual respect and empathy rather than social clout. Being surrounded by people who sincerely care for you provides a solid support system. It allows both individuals to bring their uniqueness into the relationship, creating a synergy richer than anything superficial popularity attempts to offer.

Drawing from this solid foundation, understanding the importance of earning trust naturally flows into our next discussion. Trust isn't something one can buy or demand; it is built over time through consistent actions and character. Trust becomes a crucial element where without it, even the strongest friendship pillars can crack.

Handling situations when trust is broken and becoming a person others can depend on play key roles in fortifying your circle. It opens the doors to conversations about trust that many often shy away from but adds substantial depth to any relationship. Whether handling small betrayals or grand gestures, the manner in which you address trust reinforces or shakes your friendships to their core.

By knowing what friendships should feel like and recognizing when they aren't, you can weave a meaningful network of people who truly matter. These valuable connections serve as reminders that in this vast world, our circles act as those little stars that brighten our paths. They give us strength, laughter, and a sense of belonging, making the journey infinitely worthwhile.

Trust Is Built, Not Bought

Moving from how we earn trust and provide safety for others, let's dive into the kind of friendships worth nurturing. Think about those moments when you've felt truly seen and supported. Those are the moments born out of quality friendships. Trust and reliability form the backbone of these relationships, more solid and valuable than any social media follower count. Deep, genuine connections are more impactful on your life than broad social interactions. While it might seem like there are advantages to having a large circle, it often leads to surface-level interactions, which lack the meaningful engagement that comes with a handful of close friends.

Feeling secure and authentically yourself in a friendship means you're with people who appreciate you for who you are. With a few true friends, there's space to deepen bonds and create meaningful interactions. These friendships become safe havens, places where you can express vulnerability. When life's hurdles threaten to knock you down, these connections can be the net that catches you. Imagine having a rough day and needing someone to talk to. Sure, you could post online and get tons of likes, but wouldn't a heart-to-heart chat with someone who knows your journey be more fulfilling?

This brings us to FOMO again, or the Fear of Missing Out. It's the nagging worry pushed by social media that you're left out while everyone else is living large. Many people believe that to be happy, you need to be in the thick of everything, attending every event, and maintaining broad social engagements. But the myth of FOMO can often overshadow what really matters. True friendships allow you to quit worrying about what you're missing out on because you're already part of something real. Intentional social living means choosing who you spend your energy on, and it's a liberating choice. You can visit any gathering, but where your heart feels content is where there's real connection.

These myths often tie into misconceptions about popularity and social status, especially in an age of constant connection. Popular doesn't always mean happy. Often, there's a void lurking beneath the surface. What people often overlook is that a couple of supportive friendships can outshine a string of less genuine connections. It's these quality friendships that provide support and comfort when you need them the most. For instance, during stressful life transitions, like starting a new school or job, having a stable, trusting friendship can be a beacon guiding you to calmer waters. It's the assurance that someone truly has your back.

Building such bonds isn't limited to extroverts or social butterflies. If you're shy or introverted or just beginning to establish your circle from scratch, building a supportive community is still within reach. Start by fostering connections one-on-one. Seek out individuals who share your interests or values. Join clubs, classes, or online forums that resonate with you. Often in these smaller settings, you'll find others searching for similar types of relationships. Here, depth overrules breadth, as shared experiences layer into deeper understanding and solid friendships.

With patience and authenticity, friendships evolve like carefully tended gardens. The idea is to nourish your networks with genuine interest and kindness. You often reap what you sow. If you express interest in someone's well-being, they're more likely to reciprocate, creating a cycle of support and friendship. These meaningful exchanges lay the foundation for trust, which is an essential ingredient for enduring friendships. It's the difference between knowing someone will actually pick up the phone when you call versus merely liking your photo.

Consider the scenario of someone who's navigated both shallow and deep waters. They might attend endless social gatherings, but it's always in their core circle they find solace when life becomes challenging. This inner circle is where true satisfaction lives, where shared memories and mutual growth blossom. Such friendships often weather storms, emerge stronger, and become pillars supporting life's unpredictability. That reliability and mutual reliance are rare gifts among a sea of acquaintances and cultivating those sustainable connections rewards you in manifold ways.

As you navigate the seas of connection, it's crucial to understand that friendships grow and change over time. This understanding preps you for exploring how relationships can morph, adapt, or sometimes even fade. Recognizing when friendships become toxic or drain rather than nurture you is crucial. It's equally important to embrace the emotional maturity that comes from lovingly letting these go. This acceptance and willingness to adapt your social circle as you and your surroundings change, form the natural progression of personal growth and emotional health.

As you head into exploring how these relationships evolve, keep in mind the balance between holding on and the freedom to change.

Friendships aren't stagnant; they move and shift just like you do. Understanding this will not just advance your understanding of relationships but also help you make peace with transitions. Whether a friendship strengthens or weakens, it's essential to remember that these changes reflect your journey's progression. By embracing these dynamics, you allow yourself the flexibility to grow, maintaining genuine connections that joyfully walk alongside your life path.

Armed with these insights, venture forward with openness and curiosity. Accept that friendships, like any relationship, require nurturing, patience, and sometimes reevaluations. By focusing on quality over quantity and being present in the relationships you're cultivating, you're setting the stage for a supportive community, ready to tackle whatever adventures life brings your way.

Quality Over Quantity

Navigating the realm of friendships often feels daunting, especially when transitioning into adulthood. Previously, we explored how reliability and repair build trust. Now, let's journey further into the benefits of nurturing a close-knit circle over amassing names in an address book.

Think about the times when you've wanted to be known and understood rather than merely recognized. Quality friendships offer you this chance. You're not just another face in a crowd; you're part of a conversation, a story, shared adventures. You exchange more than pleasantries, you share aspirations and fears, joys, and tears. The depth transforms acquaintances into companions who resonate with your innermost experiences.

True friendships blossom from a robust foundation of trust and dependability. While numerous casual connections might seem appealing, they rarely offer the nurturing environment necessary for personal growth. Imagine it's like gardening. A patch filled with a multitude of plants may appear abundant, but to bear fruit, each plant requires attention and care. Your close friends are these well-tended plants, thriving because you've invested time and emotion. With good care, each friendship provides shade, comfort, and nourishment in your life's garden.

Let's address the myth of FOMO, Fear of Missing Out, that shouts at you from every corner of social media. Every scrolling moment resembles missing the so-called event of the century. But here's the truth: Being everywhere often leaves us nowhere. When you try to keep up with every event, gathering, or ping on social media, you spread yourself thin. Instead, when you choose friends and activities mindfully, you curate your social life. You pick what enriches your life rather than what potentially keeps loneliness at bay. You attend a gathering not because it's happening, but because it means something to you.

Let's step further into this by thinking about practical, intentional choices. Picture a friend who always listens, truly listens, which makes you feel heard and valued. You can be that friend, too. Make eye contact, ask questions about their life, and remember the little details they share. These gestures may seem small but have a monumental impact on deepening bonds. Slowly, authentically, you cultivate a network that supports and uplifts rather than merely fills the space.

Even if you're shy, remember you're not alone in this. Plenty of people share moments of hesitation in forging new friendships. Start small. Join clubs that reflect your interests; they're full of potential friends who hold similar passions. Volunteering in community projects doesn't just help others; it's a wise way to meet like-minded folks dedicated to a cause, creating immediate common ground. This effectively stitches your social quilt; a community you can rely on.

For someone starting new, deliberate steps amplify your journey. Instead of diving into countless circles, start by identifying traits you respect in a friend. Pursue hobbies or causes that nurture these qualities, opening doors to potential friendships naturally. Social media, often a vehicle for superficial updates, can connect diverse communities. Engage thoughtfully in discussions, and gradually, authentic relationships will surface.

Another vital gem in friendship maintenance is remembering moments that matter. Celebrate milestones, big or small. Organizing a surprise party or sending a simple "I remember" note shows your friends that their lives matter to you. Personal touches are memorable for their emotional impact. Moreover, regular check-ins, even simple text messages, can fortify your connection, letting your friends know they're in your thoughts.

Beyond building new bonds, it's crucial to strengthen existing ones, especially during challenging periods. Everyone experiences life's storms. In these moments, genuine friends offer shelter. Engaging in open conversations about mental health or personal struggles not only builds trust but also normalizes vulnerability. Being vulnerable transforms relationships, allowing them to grow roots in empathy and understanding.

It's okay when friendships evolve or dwindle. Life's journey changes people, and some may walk different paths. This doesn't always mean the bond is broken; it merely adapts. Clinging to toxic friendships for the sake of nostalgia or fear of loneliness harbors no growth. As you cultivate new friendships, be mindful of the emotional waste old ones may bring. It's healthier to release negativity, leaving space for positive connections to flourish.

Leading into the next discussion, let's recognize that friendships evolve with age and circumstance. Childhood companions may not move with us into adulthood. While letting go is hard, understanding this truth sets you free to form enriched friendships later. Life constantly introduces you to new people, ideas, and values, transforming friendships into lifelong treasures or temporary lessons.

In essence, you possess the control to shape your social world. Cherish quality over quantity, understanding that those few close friendships hold the power to illuminate your path. Armed with intentional choices and genuine connections, you build a network that enhances life's quality rather than overwhelms it.

Take these insights to heart. Craft a social landscape that nurtures and helps you grow. Friends are chosen family, integral parts of our journey. You shape this journey with intentionality and care, building a life surrounded by unwavering, genuine spirits.

Growing Up and Growing Apart, And That's Okay

Having a couple of true friends counts more than a sea of acquaintances. We've heard this before, right? What's really interesting is how these core friendships affect the way we live, far beyond the clamor of superficial hangouts. Maybe you've ditched plans because FOMO tugged at your sleeve, or perhaps you've felt it sneak up on you while strolling through Instagram. But let's pause for a moment; it's about intentional living and deep connections, not about constant partying, and big numbers.

Now, let's be real. Friendships don't come with a lifetime warranty. They evolve. The people who stood by you in middle school might not walk the graduation stage with you. And that's okay. Recognizing this can release us from the guilt we sometimes feel when friendships change or fade. Growing up often means growing apart, even if no one did anything "wrong." It's a natural progression as people pursue their paths. Maybe your interests diverged. Maybe the weekly movie hangouts transformed into sporadic holiday greetings. Accepting these changes reminds us that while some friends stick around, others serve specific, valuable roles at particular moments in our lives.

Navigating these shifts can be emotional, sure, but it's an opportunity for growth. Say you've been close to someone for years, but lately, conversations feel more like obligatory exchanges or worse, battlegrounds of passive aggression. It's important here to evaluate honestly if this friendship supports who you are now. Some connections become toxic, pulling us down with comments disguised as jokes or constant undermining. We don't have to carry it just because it once was great. Letting go doesn't mean failure. It means you value your well-being and the potential for healthier relationships.

Sometimes, parting ways still feels heavy with drama. How do you drift apart without a whirlwind of bitterness? It could be as simple as having a heart-to-heart, acknowledging the distance, and deciding to engage less without hard feelings. You're not alone in this. Everyone's been there. Maybe pen a thoughtful letter or text, context-dependent of course, explaining your feelings without casting blame. The key is expressing your needs and boundaries with compassion. Approach it as you would pruning a garden. You're simply making room for what nurtures you.

Detecting whether a friendship is season-bound or destined for the long haul can prevent a lot of heartache. Some friends are meant to teach us something, brighten a period in our history, or challenge us to grow in ways we hadn't considered. You might realize this as you catch up over coffee or when you've gone through a tough season. The talk drifts seamlessly into deeper territories. Conversely, when a friendship fuels only nostalgia without new conversations, it might not be one that energizes your present or future.

Emotional growth plays a pivotal role here, too. It's like gardening your inner landscape. Imagine shedding old habits that held you back or discovering new interests that enliven your soul. We reflect these changes in our friendships; when we grow, our circles often shift naturally. Just as a tree shed leaves, we move through seasons, sometimes leaving people behind, but always allowing room for self-improvement and stronger future bonds.

Consider Jenna and Alex. Best friends since the sandbox days, they were inseparable. As they grew up, Alex found a passion for music, spending afternoons at the studio, while Jenna immersed herself in photography and volunteer work. Soon, their lives channeled different paths. They could have clung to the idea of their childhood rhythm, but instead, they chose to adapt. Instead of seeing each meet-up as a make-or-break endeavor, they cherished the moments their paths intertwined, celebrating the impact they'd had on each other's lives. They understood their friendship might not function as a day-to-day sounding board anymore, but as an ongoing, cherished chapter in their shared story.

Then there are digital connections. Our phones tie us to people across the globe, creating both a blessing and a curse. It can mean maintaining bonds overseas, but it can also extend the life support on friendships that need a gentle end. Be mindful of how these digital threads make you feel. If a text leaves you anxious rather than uplifted, it might be time to reassess its place in your life.

In Selena's case, it meant realizing that her bond with Marcus, an old roommate, remained largely through social media. Their interactions were clipped and a little strained; what once was fun became a showcase of conflict-avoidance. Selena weighed this and chose to let it fade, prioritizing genuine, in-person connections that fueled positivity. Her emotional growth thrived with people who fit her current life, like pieces in a puzzle that evolves through time.

Trust your instincts here. Balancing empathy towards friends with the requirement to prioritize your needs perfectly mirrors the maturity that navigating friendships demands. Remember, growing apart doesn't erase the narrative carved into your history. It merely turns the page, allowing space for fresh stories.

So, celebrate these changes. Nurture yourself, manage energy wisely, and know that it's natural to evolve. What matters most is the quality of your connections, finding those who encourage you and embrace who you are becoming. This journey, however winding, enriches you, building layers of resilience and understanding that no one can take away.

EPILOGUE

Embracing Social Savviness

As you close this book, take a moment to reflect on how far you have come in understanding the complexities of social media, peer pressure, anxiety, and the fear of missing out. In today's hyperconnected world, navigating these challenges requires self-awareness, resilience, and a strong sense of identity. The fact that you have taken the time to learn and grow in these areas is a testament to your commitment to a healthier, more balanced social life, both online and offline.

Being socially savvy is not about avoiding social media or rejecting peer interactions altogether; it's about using them wisely. It is about recognizing when social platforms enrich your life and when they begin to drain your energy and self-worth. It is about making choices based on your values rather than the fleeting approval of likes and comments. It is about setting boundaries, speaking up for yourself, and choosing relationships that uplift you rather than ones that cause you stress and anxiety.

The digital world will continue to evolve, and new challenges will arise, but the core principles you have learned will always apply. Prioritize your mental health. Be intentional with your time and energy. Stay true to who you are. And most importantly, seek out real, meaningful connections that go beyond screens and filters.

Your journey toward social savviness does not end here; it's a lifelong process. Continue to educate yourself, support others, and adapt to new social landscapes with confidence. If you ever feel lost, return to the lessons in this book as a guidepost to help you regain balance.

You have the tools. You have the power. Now go forward and live a life that is authentic, fulfilling, and truly connected.

The best is yet to come.

REFLECTION

Having explored the cornerstones of genuine friendships, safety, honesty, laughter, and support, alongside the importance of quality over quantity, we are now equipped with the knowledge to build deeper, more meaningful connections. Recognizing signs of thriving relationships versus those that drain can guide us in nurturing bonds that truly matter. As we move forward, let's focus on fostering authentic friendships that enrich our lives and embrace the natural evolution of these relationships. By understanding these dynamics, we create a supportive network that strengthens us through life's challenges, paving a path for personal growth and emotional well-being.

Thank you again to have come thus far and for taking the time to read this book. We (Nicci and Ben) hope you got out of it what you were looking for.

www.ingramcontent.com/pod-product-compliance
Lightning Source LLC
Chambersburg PA
CBHW071522120626
46550CB00006B/2323